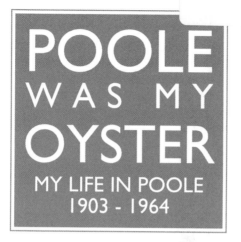

POOLE WAS MY OYSTER
MY LIFE IN POOLE
1903 - 1964

BY ERNEST BRISTOWE
EDITED BY JENNY OLIVER

POOLE HISTORICAL TRUST
1998

Copyright © Ernest Bristowe 1998
ISBN 1 873535 35 X

All rights reserved. No part of this publication may be reproduced, stored in a retrieval system or transmitted in any form or by any means without the prior permission of the copyright owner.
Prepared for publication by Ian Andrews
Designed by Graham M Smith and Andrew S Arnold.
Production by Graphic Editions, Poole.
Printed and bound in Great Britain by Biddles Limited, Guildford and King's Lynn.

Contents

	Pages
List of Illustrations	4
Introduction	7
Chapter 1	*9*
Chapter 2	*21*
Chapter 3	*31*
Chapter 4	*41*
Chapter 5	*51*
Chapter 6	*59*
Chapter 7	*69*
Chapter 8	*79*
Chapter 9	*89*
Chapter 10	*97*
Chapter 11	*107*
Chapter 12	*119*
Index	*133*

List of Illustrations

*(From the Bristowe Collection, Poole Reference Library,
except where stated otherwise)*

	Page
Poole Harbour from a postcard by Frank Richards *(J Oliver)*	Cover
Author with lamb	Cover
My parents' wedding in 1901	6
Market Street and Town Hall *(J Oliver)*	10
Poole old library and museum, South Road *(Poole Library)*	15
Launching at Lake Shipyard *(P Burt)*	19
The *"Will Everard"* at the Quay	20
The Quay *(J Oliver)*	20
Coal hoppers on the Quay, 1939	23
Diver working on the Quay wall	25
Hamworthy Ferry	27
Fishermen's Dock through the nets	30
Barbers Piles	32
Butcher's shop *(D Ridout)*	35
Guildhall Market *(S Brassfield)*	36
Poole Fire Brigade *(I K D Andrews)*	39
Near Park Gates, Poole *(J Oliver)*	42
High Street level crossing	43
Motor Park, Sandbanks *(J Oliver)*	45
The election of Alex Glassey, 1929 *(Poole Library)*	49
Camping at Sandbanks *(J Oliver)*	52
Sandbanks Ferry *(J Oliver)*	53
Banks Road, Sandbanks *(J Oliver)*	53
House boats at Stokes Lake	56
Carnival float, advertising the Regent Theatre *(Poole Library)*	59
Poole Fair in 1958	61
Poole Electric Theatre *(Poole Library)*	63
Chestnuts near Park Gates East, Poole Park *(J Oliver)*	65
The *"Bournemouth Queen"*	67
A submarine for breaking up at Ballast Quay, 1920	68
Beating the Bounds celebrations 1922 *(J Oliver)*	70

A performance by the Poole and Parkstone Operatic Society *(F Henson)* 74
Poole Adult School   75
My wedding, 1928   77
Friends' Meeting House, Interior   78
Paintresses at work   81
Gertie Gilham, 1936   82
Exhibition at Gieves Gallery, London   85
Ruth Pavely, 1936   87
"Gondolier" boats *(Poole Library)*   89
The "Monarch" off the Quay   90
The beach, Shore Road, Sandbanks *(J Oliver)*   92
Summer wear for men   93
Typhoid outbreak in Poole *(Poole Library)*   97
A German ship at Poole Quay   99
Block ships seen from the Quay   101
Bomb damage in Poole *(Poole Historical Trust)*   105
Have an air raid shelter built now *(Poole Library)*   106
The aftermath of an air raid on Bourne Valley Gasworks
   (Poole Historical Trust)   109
Air raid damage, Poole *(Poole Historical Trust)*   111
"The bend in the road"; Henbury in the snow   113
Barbed wire, Sandbanks   115
Victory celebrations, Harbour Hill Road 1945   117
Flying boat laid up at Hamworthy   118
Poole High Street and South Road, 1960   120
Blue Boar Lane, Poole, 1950's   123
New flats at Sterte, 1962   124
Arthur Browse, 1950   125
The *"Esso Tioga"* entering Poole Harbour, 1949   126
Ernest, Dorothy and Barbara   131

My parents' wedding in 1901.

INTRODUCTION

E rnest Clifford Gale Bristowe spent his 83rd birthday swimming in the sea off the Great Barrier Reef, thousands of miles from his native county of Dorset. It was a typical exploit in a life full of wide-ranging travels, interests and talents.

Descended from an old Poole family, his grandfather, William Bristowe, was a grocer and carrier in High Street and Market Street, Poole. His father, Clifford Penney Bristowe, married Charlotte Mary Gale of Salisbury, and Ernest, their first son, was born in 1903. The family lived first in Longfleet and then in Market Street where the father took over the family business.

Ernest went to Longfleet School and then to South Road School where he developed an interest in Poole history under the inspiration of his schoolmaster, H. P. Smith. Winning a scholarship to Poole Secondary School in 1915, he also became interested in nature and wild flowers with the encouragement of Mr Mockridge, the Headmaster, who was a keen botanist. Scouting and football also played a big part in his life at this time! In 1918, he was indentured to the Hamworthy Engineering Company as an engineering draughtsman, leaving five years later to take over the family haulage business. In 1928, he married Dorothy Kendall at the Quaker Meeting House in Poole and the couple went to live at Fernside Road. By now he was working for Carter, Stabler and Adams Ltd (now Poole Pottery), where he became manager.

He first took up photography in 1932 on the birth of his daughter Barbara, who was eventually to become a professional photographer herself. Another enthusiasm, caravanning, began a few years later, and was to take the family around most of the British Isles, across Europe and eventually to New Zealand and Australia. During the Second World War, he served in Civil Defence and managed two small munitions factories in Newtown. In 1946, he and Dorothy founded Bristowes Removals Ltd.

The next couple of decades were marked by an increasing love of photography, travel, geology and local and natural history, while caravanning trips provided an opportunity to develop these enthusiasms. Ernest became President of the Bournemouth Camera

Club and gained his Associateship of the Royal Photographic Society of England for his work with the Nature Photographic Society. He also began a series of illustrated lectures to various societies in Dorset and Hampshire on the subject of Poole history, the West Country, nature photography and caravanning throughout Europe. In the meantime he was developing a photographic history of Poole with the help of Dorothy and Barbara who in the early days of slum clearance, was commissioned by the Corporation to take photographs of property to be demolished which had some feature of architectural or historic interest. This collection was eventually donated to Poole Reference Library and 200 of the pictures were published by Poole Historical Trust in 'A Portfolio of Poole' in 1984.

In 1964, Ernest and Dorothy emigrated to New Zealand where Barbara was already living and, in 1980, they moved to Australia. Here he became a successful artist, drawing Dorset villages in pen and Australian scenes in pen and wash and oils, while continuing to pursue his old interests of nature, geology and travel in a new setting.

This autobiography has its origins in the series of lectures given to local societies. It is an affectionate portrait of Poole during the first half of the 20th century, through good times, hard times and two world wars. It describes a town, people, places, entertainments, activities and customs which, in spite of vast changes in the last decades, are recognisably 'ad morem villae de Poole'.

CHAPTER ONE

I was born, not in Poole, but in Blandford Forum, a town with Roman origins fourteen miles away. This relatively unimportant event in the history of England came about, I am told, because my mother wanted to be with her family for her confinement. It happened in the days when hospitals did not cater for such events, and the proceedings were supervised by a midwife. I was taken back to Poole immediately and I therefore claim to belong to the town and county of Poole.

My family lived in a modest terraced house in Denmark Road, Heckford Park, and at the age of four I started in the infants' class at Longfleet School. This was unusual because five was the required age. I remember my mother taking me there and holding my hand as I stood in a row of small children waiting to be called into the classroom, quite apprehensive that I would find learning to be difficult. In the classroom we were each given a slate and a slate pencil on which we copied a large letter 'R' which the teacher wrote on the blackboard. Next we wrote the word 'COW'. The teacher inspected each slate and said 'Good' to me. I am quite certain about these two important events in my life; I could write, and I was no longer afraid of school.

In 1910, my grandfather died, and we moved to Market Street which was dignified by the presence of the Municipal Offices, the 18th century Guildhall, and the genteel houses of Langton Terrace. One thing which intrigued me was that so many bedroom windows were filled in with brickwork. The middle one on the front of our house in Market Street had been removed, and white lines had been painted on the bricks to match the woodwork of the other windows. This was done in the 18th century to avoid paying window tax introduced by the government. In fact so many windows were filled in that the tax was removed, but the bricks remained. Through the window of the Market Street Police Station we could see about twenty cutlasses arranged in a semicircle on the wall. These we understood to be there in case of a riot, and we also knew that one of them had been used by Bobby Blues, our favourite policeman, when he fought as a cavalryman in the Boer War.

Market Street and Town Hall, Poole

There was no public transport to Longfleet and we walked or cycled the two miles to and from school. Longfleet was a Church of England school and from the age of ten we were taken on Thursday afternoons to Longfleet Church where the Reverend Canon Okes Parish preached fire and damnation to us; at least that is the impression I received. Sometimes I came away quite terrified of going to hell. The school was opposite the church and had three sections, infants, girls and boys. Another Church of England school was the Boys' National School in Lagland Street of which Mr Martin was headmaster. It had a mixed infants section whose headmistress was Miss Rattray, affectionately known as 'Rattrays'. The British School in South Road catered for Nonconformists and those with no religious affiliation. This was superseded by South Road Boys' and Girls' Schools, predictably separated by a high stone wall.

The Misses Wheatley ran a private school in Serpentine Road which was co-educational and produced some of the more worthy citizens of the town; headmasters, lawyers and professional men and women. The teaching consisted of geography learnt by heart, spelling, history, French, art, English grammar and maths. Dorothy, my wife, was a pupil there until the age of twelve and could always quote the books of the Old Testament and all the capitals and rivers of the world. She remembered chanting: 'England, London on the Thames, France, Paris on the Seine, Germany, Berlin on the Spree...' and so on.

It was always 'Italy, Rome on the Tiber' since 'Rome on the Po' was not considered suitable for such a refined establishment. Our education concentrated on the three 'R's. Each boy had to stand and read aloud a chapter of the book we were studying. Writing consisted of compositions on subjects set by the teacher, 'How I spent my holiday' or 'What I want to be when I grow up' being favourites. We learnt our tables by chanting 'Twice one are two, twice two are four...' right through to twelve times twelve.

1910 was the year in which King Edward VII died, and the next year the coronation of George V was celebrated. Poole school children assembled near to the summer house at the Seldown end of Poole Park, standing in rows in the rain to hear the mayor speak. Unfortunately, I was so far away that I had no idea what he said. We were each given a small tin containing four chocolates with a photograph of the new king and queen on the lid, and a coronation mug made of local red clay by the Dorset Pottery which operated at the southern end of Mount Street. The heads of the royal couple were embossed on the front of the mug and it was decorated with yellow clay slip, like the usual output of the pottery which included vases, bowls, ornaments and rather thick, peasant-type tableware. I kept my mug for many years, proudly displayed in a whatnot, a piece of Victorian furniture made to fit into a corner of the drawing room. Eventually, however, it went the way of a great deal of pottery; I dropped it. The pottery ceased business in the 1920's.

The year of 1910 was also notable because I saw Halley's comet. We had a large garden at the rear of the house and we all turned out after dark to see this phenomenon which had become a source of great concern to some. Some said that the comet was the cause of the King's death, or believed that it would collide with the earth and bring down Armageddon. The end of the world was predicted, people consulted Old Moore's Almanac and prayer meetings were held to ward off the danger. I was only seven, but my recollection is of a ball of light, smaller than a football, with, at its best, a long tail of sparks. It faded away after a few days.

In 1913, I went to the new South Road Boys School where Mr Prankard was the Headmaster and H. P. Smith, my form master. Mr Prankard had a profound knowledge of the works of Charles Dickens, especially 'Pickwick Papers'. Sometimes on Thursday afternoons he left his office to tell us the story of the Pickwick Club, Sam Weller and his father Toby who mixed up their 'v's and 'w's. 'Quite right Samivel, me boy, spell it with a wee'. It was great stuff compared with the conventional, stereotyped learning, and opened up an interest in reading which has never left me.

Our education was basic; most of the subjects were elementary by today's standards. History consisted mainly of battles, particularly those which ended in victory for our side or in which our soldiers were very brave. If we lost it was usually because of external factors such as the snow in the Crimea, or through dirty tricks on the part of the enemy like the Black Hole of Calcutta, Harold being shot in the eye at Hastings, or the Boers fighting and running away instead of standing in lines to be shot down! Somehow it did not seem fair that Amundsen had reached the South Pole before Captain Scott. The most splendid stories were of Trafalgar, Waterloo, the defeat of the Spanish Armada and the charge of the Light Brigade. Together we shouted Tennyson's lines: 'Cannon to right of them, / Cannon to left of them, / Cannon behind them, volleyed and thunder'd'.. and from 'The Burial of Sir John Moore': 'We buried him darkly at dead of night, / The sods with our bayonets turning', (the last line causing some hilarity among the more ribald characters).

Around this time, H. P. Smith, wrote a history of Poole for the local paper, the Poole Guardian, appearing at weekly numbers at 1d a copy. We were encouraged to cut out the articles and paste them into an exercise book. Mr Gould, the newsagent, provided the school with newspapers and when the series finished, three monitors, of whom I was one, had to return the money and the remaining papers to him. The money was hopelessly short, I think by as much as 1s 10d which we had failed to collect. I was quite terrified that such a huge sum was missing. Mr Gould, suspicious that some boys had not paid for their papers, was adamant about payment, and so H. P. Smith paid the difference.

Every Thursday evening, H. P. Smith and Mr Prankard took about six of us on bicycles to see some local historical site, the earthworks at Badbury Rings and Dudsbury, the round and long barrows of the ancient inhabitants of Britain, or one of the Roman Roads that ran through East Dorset. From H. P. Smith we learnt about Harry Paye, the Poole pirate, located the old water gate off the Quay, and traced the site of the town gate in Towngate Street.

The outbreak of war shattered our peaceful existence. Recruits for Kitchener's army lined up in the playground of South Road School, were shouted at by Sergeant Major Pitt from the nearby drill hall, and marched away to the cheers of the crowd, little knowing what awaited them in Flanders. In spite of the anticipation, Britain was unprepared for war. Volunteers who rushed to join up were put into bell tents in huge camps. Winter came quickly after the outbreak of war. Influenza and pneumonia struck, and many found themselves in wounded blue, a uniform that was really the prerogative of those wounded in battle. There were no khaki uniforms for the early volunteers and they were given second-hand dress uniforms, red tunics, blue trousers with a red stripe and matching caps. Every Sunday troops came on day leave from Wareham and Bovington, to be entertained by the civilian population. The churches prepared teas for them and liberal families would invite a couple to Sunday dinner. We had two young men each Sunday for several months. They soon went to France but the entertaining continued for the whole of the war. The Royal Engineers were stationed at Sterte, and a soldiers' club was opened for them by Skinner Street Congregational Church. Men came every evening for billiards, table tennis and refreshments. We youngsters also joined in, and after the war the idea was continued for young people.

During the war we learnt the National Anthems of the allies and sang them in unison. It did not matter if you could not sing in tune; we all had to sing and woe betide anyone who did not. To teach us the tonic sol-fa, the teacher would hold up his hand giving the eight symbols while we all sang 'do, ray, me', supposedly in unison. As he gestured up and down the scale, we were supposed to hit the right note but it was very much of a hit and miss affair. 'Do' was a clenched fist level with his waist (bottom C), or at eye level, (top C). A forefinger pointed heavenward represented 'Te', a source of derision for some of the non-caring participants.

On Oakapple Day in May, I used to wear an oakapple in my lapel to commemorate Charles II's escape from Worcester when he hid in the oak tree at Boscobel. (It had to be an oakapple; an acorn would not do). On Empire Day we saluted the flag and sang 'Rule Britannia' and 'Heart of Oak'. In the schools there was great rivalry between the British Lions and the National Tigers, which usually ended in a shouting match; 'The National Tigers climbed the wall, The British Lions downed them all', or vice versa, depending which side you were on. Sometimes a stone or two was thrown and in school both headmasters were liable to a certain amount of violence from recalcitrant pupils. These were the days of corporal punishment and it was not uncommon for an irate parent to visit the school because his son had been thrashed. The cane was used to keep us in order, even at secondary school. Three cuts of the cane across tightened shorts left three black and blue lines which were there for a long time. In the elementary schools it was the hand that took the punishment, with an occasional beating. Five and six-year-olds could expect a rap over the knuckles with a round ruler for the slightest misdemeanour. In 1913, three of my ten-year-old classmates from Longfleet School were sentenced to six strokes of the birch, administered by a hefty policeman, for putting sleepers on the railway line at Whitecliff. They admitted that it hurt.

Every year the Poole Corporation and the Dorset County Council each gave twelve scholarships at Poole Secondary School for boys and twelve for girls, the candidates all coming from the National and British schools including Parkstone and Branksome, and from towns and villages as far away as Swanage. The scholarship was for three years, but most pupils stayed for another two years to take the Oxford Local Senior Examination which excused matriculation. In 1915, I won a town scholarship for three years to Poole Secondary school at Seldown, and was told to go along with pencil, pen, ruler and rubber. I did quite well for about two years, but then gave all I had to football and cricket. One of my reports said: 'He would do better if he brought his football enthusiasm into school'. My mother was not pleased.

In spite of this inattention to things scholastic, I enjoyed school and wanted to learn and so became an avid reader. When I was twelve I won first prize for the whole of East Dorset in a scripture examination based on the Acts of the Apostles, but I did not continue with this worthy aspect of literature. I preferred 'The Pickwick Papers', 'Oliver Twist', 'King Solomon's Mines' and 'The Adventures of Sherlock Holmes'. At the age of twelve, I joined the Poole Free Library and read Henty, Fenimore-Cooper, Mark Twain and Jules Verne. I preferred 'The Scout', (for which Herbert Carter sometimes wrote) to other titles like 'The Gem' or 'The Magnet' with Billy Bunter and Tom Cherry. Later it was Sir Walter Scott, Charles Dickens and Joseph Conrad, Captain Scott, Shackleton and Peary.

The Library was given to the town in the 1880's by John J. Norton, following the tradition of Carnegie, the great American philanthropist, who sponsored hundreds of library buildings throughout Britain. Johnny Norton was a successful timber merchant importing deals from the Baltic, and operating from timber yards in Towngate street and West Shore. Originally, the library had a huge screen covered with numbers representing the books, shown in blue if they were on the shelves or in red if they were on loan. The public were not allowed to browse through the stock and could only choose books by their titles. This system seemed very complicated to me at the age of twelve and at times the staff found it difficult to keep the board up to date. Eventually, the library stock was put on open access and at last we could handle the books. The reading room stocked newspapers and magazines but at one time it became something of a doss-house for hopeless characters who simply wanted to sit there and go to sleep. A change of librarian put a stop to this.

The building also housed the museum, which was once described by one of His Majesty's Inspectors as being the second worst in Britain. Museums are always faced with having to accept items from

Poole old library and museum, South Road.

people who want to dispose of them, and later to discard the gifts without hurting the feelings of the donors. Certainly, this museum was very full, but everything must have been of interest at some time. Years later, I was involved in an interesting exercise when our removal company had to transport a collection of native weapons and artefacts that had come from Nigeria. They had been in the museum since the opening, the gift of a Poole man who had been in the colonial service. We catalogued the items, numbered them, and delivered them to the Nigerian Embassy in London. The Ambassador told me that they were better than those in his country's possession. The gymnasium was also housed in the library building, and in the early 1920's, a flourishing club met once a week to use the apparatus. The boy scouts also used it for several years.

Apart from reading, I became interested in natural history. Mr Mockridge, the Headmaster, was a keen botanist with a love of British wild flowers which he encouraged us to collect. His desk at morning assembly was covered with jam jars full of water and specimens that we had brought in. The names and locations of the finds were recorded by monitors, and I became an enthusiastic collector. The standard reference book was John's 'Flowers of the Field' which cost 8s 6d, and I kept my copy for sixty years. The school's greatest find was Sysirinchium Augustifolium, found by Margaret Hannaford at Hamworthy. It had probably come from Newfoundland in the ballast of a sailing ship.

Sport, however, was my main passion. We had a problem with the school playing field which was very rough as far as grass was concerned and liable to flooding. Its only amenities were two soccer goal posts without nets. The school had one football team which played in Poole Park. Form football consisted of A form playing B form, which gave us about fourteen or fifteen a side. We played in our school clothes, which was a cause of concern to some mothers. Football boots were mostly unheard of, and generally speaking everyone just followed the ball round the field.

I felt that a pair of football boots was an absolute necessity and was excited to see a string of them, grey in colour and complete with leather studs, hanging outside Morton's boot shop, priced at 2s 6d. After managing to extract 2s 6d from my father, I hurried to the shop only to find that the boots at half a crown were too small, and I needed 3s 6d; so I had to beg for another shilling. The boots were my most treasured possession, and because of them I was made captain of 2A's fourteen (or sometimes fifteen) runabouts. I even managed a pair of football shorts. When I was selected for the school eleven the following year, the problem was a shirt in the school colours of green and yellow halves. There were none for sale in the shops, but Les Norrish found one in the school coal hole, dirty and torn, and my mother washed it and repaired the tear with a piece off the tail. The shirt and the boots were to me at fourteen a great source of pride.

I held my place in the team for two seasons, as we played Bournemouth School, Bournemouth Collegiate in Meyrick Park; Wimborne Grammar and, to fill the season, Longfleet Rovers. There was also a team from Branksome who called themselves the Whisky and Sodas, besides old boys' teams of soldiers on leave from the army. The latter games were good because we had a tea in the main hall with cream cakes, an unheard of luxury in wartime.

As the war progressed, with disasters in France and shipping losses, food became scarce and everything became a matter of survival. All the masters had gone to war except the headmaster, Mr Mockridge. They were replaced by Mr Cleaver and the Rev. Mr Crick, two elderly gentlemen, together with about eight ladies, some of whom came straight from college to teach a mob who were sometimes virtually uncontrollable.

In 1915, we were told that Holton Heath Cordite Factory needed acorns, (in competition with pig farmers who needed them for feed). We never really found out why they were wanted, but it was suggested that they were to be used experimentally for human consumption, or for feeding to bugs and insects in some process to do with cordite. The most plausible explanation was that acetate (or it might have been acetone), was to be extracted from them. No-one ever told us but whatever the reason, the school responded to the appeal. Boys and girls spent their weekends collecting acorns and brought them to school on Monday mornings where each class had several bushel baskets ready. It was a splendid sight. The Swanage train boys struggled along the Ladies' Walking Field with hundredweights; they had a much better environment for collecting than we did. Town boys went out on bicycles and were limited to a sack tied on the back carrier and one on the handlebars. Those collected were paid for by the factory, and the money went to the Red Cross. It was much more exciting than Latin but not as good as football or cricket. One Saturday, the whole school was invited to collect acorns from the grounds of Upton House which belonged to the Llewellyn family. About a hundred of us went along, but I found two magnificent sweet chestnut trees laden with fruit and my acorn contribution suffered considerably.

The same year, at the age of twelve, I became a boy scout. One of my first jobs was as a messenger with two others at Poole Railway Station, meeting the hospital trains carrying wounded from France. They usually arrived at around midnight, having stopped at every station from Southampton, off-loading as many as the hospitals could take. At Poole they were met by doctors, nurses and stretcher bearers, and then moved on to Dorchester. They travelled at night so that the general public would not see the extent of the casualties. The only trains that came in daylight were those carrying German wounded, guarded by British troops with fixed bayonets. They looked very ill and grey.

Wartime rationing was very severe. Once a week I queued from six thirty in the morning until eight o'clock when the Maypole Dairy in the High Street opened, to buy half a pound of margarine. I also searched the town for potatoes and was sometimes able to buy some for three pence a pound. We ate artichokes, which mother boiled like potatoes, and the one available cereal was semolina, a kind of flaked corn, which my mother cooked like rice pudding because there was not much else you could do with it.

One evening there was a commotion in Market Street and people gathered around the steps of the Guildhall in response to a rumour that a Zeppelin had bombed Southampton and was on its way to attack Poole. We looked skyward where the moon shone intermittently through a bank of dark clouds. Just what we were to do was unclear. Presumably we would have scattered if anything had happened, since Poole had no defence against air attack. However, nothing happened. We gossiped for a while and then went back to bed.

During the war a shortage of steel led to experiments with concrete ships, and a shipyard was established at Lake on the Hamworthy shore to build them, completing a concrete barge in 1918. The launching day attracted a large crowd with shipyard workers and their families being invited to a tea. There were so many people that the hall had to operate two sittings, and most people wanted to be at the first one. The scouts were supposed to collect tickets but a number of men gatecrashed into the first sitting, pushing us aside. The barge, bedecked with flags, was successfully launched, the first and last time that I have ever seen a launching. This concrete vessel was the only one built because the war finished before the next keel could be laid.

The scouts were also called upon to help with wounded soldiers who were survivors from a hospital ship torpedoed in the English Channel. They were brought in by French fishing boats and taken to Cornelia hospital on horse-drawn drays, belonging to Coastlines. On another occasion we were on duty when survivors of a torpedoed merchant ship landed at the Quay. They had been in the water for several hours but gave three cheers as they came ashore, and were taken off to be reclothed by Dolph Shutler. I practised my schoolboy French on one of the rescuers, asking if the 'sous-marin' had been sunk, but he shook his head.

Later, the town contributed its share to the war when it became a base for Scottish herring drifters which had been converted to mine sweepers. In 1916, a fleet of them sailed off to the Dardanelles, carrying among their crews, teenagers from Poole and Weymouth as signallers. These were ex sea scouts who had learnt their craft practising Morse and semaphore with flags along the Quay. On a

Lake shipyard

moonlit night we were on the beach at Sandbanks as they sailed from the main Quay, sirens sounding, all lights showing, and their coal-burning boilers pouring black smoke over the peaceful waters of the main channel. They passed the Bell Buoy off Brownsea in line astern and were soon lost to sight off Old Harry Rocks on the first stage of a journey quite hazardous for such small craft. This journey would take them creeping along the coasts of France and Spain, (the hunting grounds of Harry Paye), past Gibraltar and through the Mediterranean and Aegean to Asia Minor.

The war ended for us with a bonfire on Constitution Hill, organised by Mr Conway, the School Attendance Officer. About fifty scouts were placed around the seaward slopes of the hill, each armed with a sea rescue flare and a king sized match. At the discharge of a gun, each boy struck his match on the end of the flare, which he then lit and held high at arms length. I managed to burn myself, but it was well worth it. The bonfire was about twenty feet high and as it burned fiercely, must have been visible from the Purbeck Hills to the Isle of Wight, a successor to the beacons lit in the time of Henry VIII, (except that those of the amorous king were lit to warn of possible invasion instead of the end of a war). The crowd cheered, sang and danced, and some were roaring drunk as another fire appeared on the Purbeck Hills, tiny at first and then, like ours, spreading to the sky.

The Quay, Poole.

The 'Will Everard' at the Quay

CHAPTER TWO

We lived not far from the harbour and as a child I used to spend as much time as possible along the Quay with my father, extending my visits as I grew older. I was fascinated by the activity, the foreign ships and sailors, the cargoes, the grimy colliers, the horse-drawn traffic and the opening of the iron bridge. In those days, when people lived reasonably slowly, the prosperity of Poole came from the port, the quayside merchants, and the traders and shopkeepers who conducted their business within a mile of the Quay.

There was always a lot to see. I used to watch particularly for the three masted wooden barquentines coming in to the harbour. They would lower their t'gallants and topsails off Old Harry Rocks and wait there for the steam tug to bring them in to line the quays, their ensigns flying from the stern and their sails drying in the wind. These ships brought timber from the Baltic, coal from Newcastle and oil cake from Liverpool, and often sailed out loaded with local clay. Brown-sailed Thames barges with a two-man crew brought cement from London and loaded up with clay destined for Stoke on Trent via Liverpool. Hoys and packets traded with the Channel Islands, bringing tomatoes and potatoes and returning with general cargo. Tiny ships brought French onion men from Roscoff, and smoky colliers brought Newcastle coal for the gasworks which was unloaded by transporter.

Although steam ships were generally replacing sail, Scandinavian sailing ships still came, their tall raking masts, spars and rigging rising high above the warehouses, public houses and chandlers' stores that lined the Quay. There was always the chance of seeing the tug boat bringing in a sailing ship from the Channel, her decks piled high with deals and her Plimsoll line showing that she was not overloaded. I would have loved to have helped with the mooring ropes which were dragged on to the Quay and looped over the iron bollards or tied to large iron rings. The anchor would crash into the water to slow the ship's approach to the Quay, dragging its chain through the hawse hole with a glorious sound. It was thrilling to see the men go aloft to furl the sails, and, once the ship was moored, slung over the side to paint ship.

Sometime in 1912, a great white ship registered in Finland came in with deals for Johnny Norton, whose yards were in West Shore and Towngate Street near the station. After some shouting, manoeuvring and pushing by the tug, she tied up to the bollards opposite Burden's, the ships' chandlers, close to the Harbour Office and Customs House, but leaving enough room for the Hamworthy ferry boat to reach its steps under her stern. Her bowsprit pointed skyward, sheltering the figure-head, a buxom lady with flowing blonde hair. A gangway was pushed on to the Quay and her captain, in a peaked cap and pea jacket, stood on the poop with the helmsman. I watched two customs men go aboard, together with a man in a bowler hat, carrying a sheaf of papers, who probably represented Norton's. Within an hour, carts arrived with their patient horses, and unloading commenced. The timber carts had four wheels with a long pole between them to suit the length of the deals. Nose bags were put on the horses and they munched away contentedly, swishing their tails to keep the flies away.

Cargoes were brought up out of the hold by hand-wound winches, and dock labourers then carried them on their backs to the waiting carts and drays. Running down planks from the ships' sides with bags of coal, cake or grain or piles of deals on their shoulders, the dockers achieved the incredible total of thirty or forty tons a man a day. Wages were governed by the number of ships in port and the labour available, but probably amounted to about twenty five shillings a week. One cargo requiring much hard labour was the clay which came from the famous ball clay mines near Wareham, owned by Pike Brothers. It was shipped across the harbour by barge from the wooden piers of Goathorn at the 'back of Brownsea' where only shallow rowing boats and sailing dinghies dared venture along the narrow channels. At Poole it had to be transferred to ocean-going ships. Men dug the clay from the barges and shovelled it into baskets which were hand-winched to the deck of the ship so that the clay could be dumped into the ship's hold. The whole operation took two or three weeks, according to the weather. If it rained, work stopped, hatches were placed over the holds and covers over the barges, and the men drew no pay.

Horses, carts and hand trolleys criss-crossed the Quay to the warehouses, crossing the railway line with its trucks which were loaded in the same way as the carts and drays, by human labour. Small tank engines, the 'Havre' and the 'St. Malo', pulled the trucks round to the Quay in the morning and took them away in the late afternoon along West Shore to the station yard, preceded by a railway man carrying green and red flags. In later years from the window of Carter's Pottery, I often saw children raiding the railway trucks, two throwing out the coal, two sacking it up, and one on look-out. They had a clear view each way of any approaching persons of authority, and police in motor cars were unheard of.

One railway employee performed a most improbable job. Every day he walked from the goods yard to East Quay, armed with an iron bar one and a half inches wide, bent at the end to form a scraper, which would just fit into the gap between the two rails, and pushing a small two-wheeled cart. His job was to see that the line was not blocked, particularly along the Quay where coal used to fall from the trucks and carts. He also carried a sack and collected any lumps of coal that were worth saving, presumably as one of his perks. Sometimes he had the bonus of larger lumps which had fallen into the

Coal hoppers on the Quay, 1939.

road due to the overloading of the railway trucks. This menial, but presumably essential task he performed for several years. Certainly, no train ever came off the track because of blocked rails, and it was a job for life if he wanted it because when he left the lines clear at the end of the day, they would inevitably be blocked again the next.

The coal merchants of Poole had two enormous iron structures which were placed on the Quay when a coal ship berthed. They were about twenty feet high with a hopper at the top. Several hundredweight of coal were hoisted from the ship and emptied into the hopper from which they hurtled downwards, passing through various sized screens for grading. Coal dust covered the Quay and its buildings and caused havoc at the pottery where fine tableware developed spots as the dust settled on glazes and slipware, and even became fired into the clay. There seemed to be no way that the coal merchants could be made to scrap the method. The coal was sprayed with water but this seemed only to be a way to make the coal weigh more, and customers were paying for water at coal prices. After a few years, however, the coal ships were taken from the main Quay to Hamworthy, where a transporter operated the unloading, and Hamworthy received the dust instead of Poole. To add to the congestion on the Quay, 'Kinson' Pottery ran a steam traction engine drawing two trucks to collect coal and take it along West Shore to the 'top of town'. The route ran over the level crossing, past the Round House, then up Longfleet Road to the *Shah of Persia* and on to the pottery near Sea View. The engine always left a trail of black smoke in its wake.

I always enjoyed watching the moving bridge in operation. Often a tug boat would slow and stop off the Ballast Quay, sounding its siren for the bridge to open. Archie, (we never knew his surname), would start to wind the winch, incurring the wrath of a carter who had just failed to get across. His vocabulary could always cope with the situation and invariably there would be a shouting match: 'Get a move on, Archie'. 'You wait. I've only got one pair of hands', at which he seemed to work more slowly. A toll was charged to cross the bridge, sixpence a week to walk over, with a graduated scale for motor vehicles, horse-drawn carts, cyclists, flocks of sheep or cattle, down to bath chairs. Then there was the rare occasion on a stormy winter's day when I heard the three warning rockets and rushed to the lifeboat house in time to see the lifeboat thundering down the slipway, ten oarsmen aboard and the steersman standing in the stern, all of them protected by oilskins, sou'westers and cork life-jackets.

Other ships operating from the Quay were the cream-funnelled paddle steamers of Messrs Cozens of Weymouth, the *'Empress'*, the *'Victoria'*, and the *'Emperor of India'*. Their competitors were the South

Coast Company who ran the *'Brodrick Castle'*. the *'Stirling Castle'* and the *'Princess Helena'*. There was intense rivalry between the two companies which kept prices to a minimum. Sometimes we could go to Swanage on a Saturday excursion for one shilling return. The Poole Town Band played all the way out and back, and at Swanage we would buy a basket of strawberries for sixpence and walk up to the great globe. On one occasion, two rival vessels reached the harbour mouth together and raced each other up the main channel, the passengers cheering and encouraging the captains to greater effort, sirens blasting and black smoke pouring from the funnels. Both captains had their licenses suspended.

Mr Chislett was the Harbour Master and kept a stern eye on happenings along the Quay, making sure that ships were berthed in the right place. With his binoculars he scanned the water, and reported hooligans throwing stones into the harbour. He and his crew checked the light buoys, the light in line and the channel stakes, took depth soundings and controlled the work of the dredger and the three hoppers, *'Hop'*, *'Skip'* and *'Jump'*, which were towed out to the channel to dispose of the mud. These were later superseded by *'Tweedledum'* and *'Tweedledee'*.

Once I spent a whole morning watching a diver repairing the Quay wall. He went down wearing a large copper helmet with an oval glass plate in the front, a baggy waterproof suit, and lead weights on

Diver working on the Quay wall.

25

his boots. Two rubber pipes connected him to a hand pump which was worked by two men turning a wheel to give him air. When he wanted to come to the surface, he pulled on a rope to signal and then laboriously climbed a ladder on to a flat barge where he sat in a chair while his helmet was removed.

Over the years many people fell over the edge of the Quay, either accidentally or deliberately. Under the portico of the Harbour Office hung a life belt, a rope and a long pole with a hook on the end for this sort of emergency. I once saw a motor truck dashing along the Quay with a man standing on the running board, holding the pole. He was on his way to the rescue of a woman who was in the water near the gas works transporter. Harry Davis, landlord of the *Jolly Sailor*, dived into the harbour thirty seven times to the rescue of people in the water, and was awarded the Royal Humane Society Medal. On one occasion, there was a great deal of excitement when a motor truck was reported stolen and tyre marks seemed to suggest that it had been driven into the water near Burden's, the ships' chandlers. Divers spent the whole afternoon searching for the truck, but without success. I waited, armed with a camera, hoping for an addition to my history of Poole, but in vain; they found nothing.

As children, we liked to cross to Hamworthy by the ferry which dated back to the time of Elizabeth I. Two men took it in turns to row, half a day each. One of them was Tinker Emberley who patiently did his stint, morning or afternoon, but his mate was not very obliging. On wet days, he was inclined to skulk in his hut, turning a blind eye to his customers waiting on the Poole side. This led to shouting, arguments, and threats to report him. Later, George Davis, a one-legged ex-seaman, and his son ran a much more efficient service. The exciting times of the day were just before 8 am. and 1 pm. when employees of the Hamworthy Engineering Company arrived. They were docked half an hour's pay if they failed to clock in on time and consequently the ferry was loaded to the gunwales. The boat was wide and men used to jump from the Quay, desperate to arrive on time. Occasionally someone would fall into the harbour, and I have been in the boat with the water within an inch or so of the top of the rail.

At the junction of Ferry Road and Hamworthy Road stood Godwin's slaughter house from where the shrieks of pigs could be heard as they were manhandled. Sometimes one would escape, invariably making for the water, chased by the slaughter men, bloody and brandishing sticks. As the road was narrow, people would scatter into the shipyard nearby or into the open space outside the *Shipwright's Arms*. I once saw a terrified animal fall over the Quay, and its pursuers trying to get it into the ferry. The building later became a bone factory, supplied by truckloads of bones arriving from the local

Hamworthy ferry.

butchers every day. The factory produced bone meal and fat for tallow and the smell was appalling. It permeated the entire locality and even wafted over to the main Quay. Protests and petitions were without avail as it was considered to be an essential industry and would have been equally undesirable if located elsewhere. It finally disappeared in the 1930's.

The shores of the harbour have often been modified by man. When the London and South Western Railway extended its line to link Bournemouth with the Dorchester line, it built an embankment from Whitecliff across the shallow water of the harbour by the side of Pitwines, part of the Gas Company's land. It enclosed a stretch of water that became the salt water lake of Poole Park, and the path between the lake and the line became known as the 'Bunny'. Lock gates were installed in a channel under the line and these could be operated every few months on an ebb-tide to drain the lake (although not very efficiently). Mr Harker Curtis contended that the gates were hung upside down and used to write periodically to the *Poole Herald* pointing out the fault. From its early days, the lake was a great asset to the park with rowing and sailing boats for hire, paddle boats for children and later an enclosed pond for model yachts. In a hard winter, ice would form, although it was never hard enough for skating. The fresh water lake, however, usually provided thick ice for sliding and skating most winters.

As well as building fighting ships and breeding pirates and smugglers, Poole has always been a fishing port as indicated in the old doggerel: 'If Poole were a fish pool/And the men of Poole fish/There'd be food for the devil/And fish for his dish.' A specially designed boat was produced to suit the harbour conditions and until the first world war the fishing fleet worked under sail. It could only get to sea when the tide and wind were favourable and this gave the fish time to breed on the mud flats of the harbour. The boats trawled in the harbour channels and on the sand banks off Bournemouth and Christchurch.

As a variation, six men and a boat-owner, like Jacob Matthews, would use a seine net or tuck net, as it was known locally, along the beaches of Poole Bay. They rowed the four miles from Poole, using a small sail if the wind was favourable. The net was put out in a semicircle and then hauled in by hand, the men trudging up the beach wearing a corset of waterproof oilskin to which they attached the line, thereby taking the weight of the net on their backs. It was very hard work for little return, the catch being divided into eight parts, one for each rower, one for the owner and one for the boat. In 1911 or 1912, the net would bring in large numbers of small fry, plaice, sole, halibut and brill about one inch long, many of which would be suffocated in the cod end of the net. The fishermen would take all saleable fish but it was difficult to save the miniature ones. Some were collected by small children and put into buckets filled with water, where they invariably died. After the war, paraffin and petrol engines were installed in the boats which were then able to trawl the harbour in more or less any weather, as the tide and wind were of no consequence. Within ten years, the fish were decimated and by the 1930's, a tuck net would be lucky to bring in twenty fish, with no miniature ones at all, due to over-fishing.

As a child I spent a lot of my spare time on the Quay, fishing for plaice, dabs and whiting, or crossing to Hamworthy to dig bait and watch the building of a wooden schooner, 'The Pride of the West', near the Shipwright's Arms. Later I caught the tiny, thick-lipped wrasse from the wreck at the Haven side of the harbour entrance; their scales shone with a brilliance that surely out-matched Joseph's coat of many colours. Using a green cotton line and a small hook baited with lug worms, dug at low tide at Stoke's Lake, I graduated to more edible species, the red-spotted plaice, the lemon sole, the humble, dark-backed flook and the school bass that invaded the harbour in the summer months. Wading in shallow water, I caught flooks in Sou' Deep between Shell Bay and Brownsea Island by 'tickling', carefully drawing the fingers along the sand until one was felt and then grabbed.

Eels were abundant, and Shell Bay cockles and winkles were the best in the world. Poole sprats arrived immediately after Christmas when very few people wanted them, the fishing fleet coming in laden down to the gunwales. Anyone could buy a bucketful for sixpence. We fried them as they were with a little salt and as they were so oily there was no need for any cooking fat. Alternatively we could souse them in vinegar and bake them in the oven. The trouble was that a bucketful was enough for the season. The fishermen caught them with no hope of selling them and I have seen boats laden with sprats that were slowly rotting. They were eventually sold to Bobby Arnold for three pence a bushel to plough into his farm at Upton. He had so many seagulls around that it was said the birds did more for his land than the sprats.

Oysters thrived on the mud flats in the harbour and had been dredged for centuries. The famous Whitstable beds were formed by a cargo of the succulent shellfish that was scattered when a Poole ship foundered in the eighteenth century at the mouth of the Thames. There were however times when the oysters needed cleansing and were relaid on the sandy beds at Arne on the western shores of the harbour to cleanse themselves. The responsibility for them was entrusted to the two Orchard brothers who received the shellfish from the fishermen, relaid them, collected them, and sacked them for sale. There was also an out-of-harbour oyster that was very much larger than normal, and unwanted by the connoisseurs, although excellent fried in butter. The Orchards refused to accept these oysters and the fishermen then brought them to Ernest Kendall, (later my father-in-law), arguing that they had been taken in the harbour. To prove the point one way or another, test dredging was carried out at the place where they were supposed to have been found. No test ever found them, but as a result we sometimes acquired oysters to eat.

For us the best shellfish was the cockle that thrived on the sandy shore inside the harbour from Harvey's to the Haven and along the in-harbour shore of Shell Bay. We used to sight them by the two small eyes that shone through the sand. By the 1920's the cockle had almost disappeared as public transport brought more and more people to experience the delights of Sandbanks. In the words of Jack Lovell, the one-legged owner of the Shell Bay cafe, 'The cockle doesn't stand a dog's chance'. Whelk and cockle stands operated outside some of the public houses on the Quay, but whelks were so tough as to be inedible to a small boy. For the gourmet, however, twelve whelks and a pint of beer was the normal intake. The one shellfish that was fascinating but uneatable was the razor clam which inhabited the beach on the Channel side of Sandbanks. It was about six inches long and thrust itself above the sand, but disappeared rapidly as one approached and was impossible to dig out.

Fishermen's Dock through the nets.

CHAPTER THREE

Looking back, it is quite obvious that large numbers of people at the beginning of the century were living on a pittance. Their future in old age would be to live with their children, or be incarcerated in the workhouse in Longfleet, where men and women were separated and worked for six shillings a week and their keep. This, the only source of social security, was run by a Board of Guardians elected by the ratepayers. In spite of hard times, people generally accepted their lot. They lived in streets like Bowling Green Alley, (which had not seen grass for a hundred years), Dear Hay Lane, Barber's Piles, Caroline Row, Oak Alley, Cinnamon Lane and Old Orchard, whose delightful names belied their reality. Strangers were rare and the rent collector who called once a week was the only regular visitor. Sometimes the shout of 'Look out! Here comes old Conway' warned of the approach of the school attendance officer, coming to enquire about a truant. Mr Conway, a sturdy red-faced gentleman with a white beard, was quite capable of stopping any boy or girl who looked as though they should have been at school, and it was not uncommon for parents to be taken to court for allowing truancy. The cottages were crowded together as they had been for hundreds of years, one building supporting another, and no two alike. Most of them had a Purbeck stone step at the front door which was cleaned several times a week by scrubbing. The doors opened on to alleys or narrow streets where washing was often hung out from house to house. Aspidistras were displayed in the front windows but I never saw one in flower. Most houses had a small back yard where fowls could be kept in pens, and rabbits in hutches for the children. There was usually a communal tap and toilet.

Before the advent of the gas cooker, every kitchen was equipped with an iron range, consisting of an oven and hot water boiler with room for three iron saucepans on the top. Once the range was really hot it would burn coke, which was cheaper than coal and could be bought from the coal merchants or direct from the Bournemouth Gas and Water Company's yard in East Street. On Saturday mornings, the inhabitants of the Quay area could be seen with sack trucks, go-karts, prams, even bicycles laden with sacks of coke. The range would burn

Barber's Piles.

almost continuously and there was always a kettle on the hob. The iron range was gradually replaced by the gas cooker, and oil lamps by gas jets and then by gas mantles, on a penny in the slot or later a shilling in the slot meter. It was a sign of prosperity to have the meter removed and to receive a bill from the gas company. Electric light came to many houses in the late 1920's. The streets were lit by gas lamps in which a pilot light burnt all day. At dusk the lamp lighter came by on his bicycle, armed with a long stick with a bent wire on the end. With this he skilfully hooked a large ring at the base of the lamp to light it while still riding. In case of difficulty he carried a ladder strapped to the bicycle. At daylight next day he returned to put the light out. I always admired the lampposts which were made of cast iron, painted green and decorated with dolphins. In the 1950's I bought one for two pounds and placed it in my garden. Granny Cousins, a very old lady who wore a white apron and bonnet, was the town's 'knocker-up'. Armed with a long pole she would tap at a bedroom window to wake a sleeper for sixpence a week.

The way of life also had a spiritual warmth, because many people enjoyed their religion. Sunday schools were crowded, morning and afternoon, if only to get the children out of the way. Some joined in time to go on the annual Sunday school treat. In Lagland Street, a special Bethel Mission was held for the poor under the Superintendent, Mr Edward Short. At harvest festival people sang: 'All good gifts around us are sent from heaven above', or 'The rich man in his castle, the poor man at his gate, He made them high and lowly and ordered their estate', with an acceptance of the status quo.

On Sunday mornings, the Salvation Army marched around the town from the citadel in Fish Street, and in the evening they played at Topp's Corner. Complete with flag bearer, concertina and tambourines, the brass band played 'Throw out the Lifeline', supported by loud 'Hallelujahs'. Meanwhile, the Plymouth Brethren preached on the corner opposite the Wesleyan chapel. People walked sedately to church or chapel, carrying their bibles. On Sunday afternoon, the usual form of relaxation was to walk up the High Street and through the park in one's Sunday clothes, feeding the swans on the lake, or the peacocks and pheasants in the bird sanctuary. The energetic walked round the lake by way of the 'Bunny' to Whitecliff and then back through the park.

These of course were the days of shillings and pence when pennies, half pennies and farthings were regular currency. Items in draper's shops could be priced at nine and eleven pence three farthings and the farthing handed over as change. Tiny shops served the inhabitants of Poole with bread, milk, tea, (Horniman's for the connoisseur), cocoa, biscuits loose in tins, eggs, bacon, tobacco and boiled sweets. Food was bought in minuscule quantities: one rasher, one egg and half a loaf of bread for father's evening meal. The favourite cigarettes were Woodbines which could be bought one at a time. For the sickly there were 'Dr. Potter's Pink Pills for Pale People', cod liver oil to give strength, and Scott's Emulsion for colds. The shops were usually cottages with the front window enlarged, displaying dummy packet of cigarettes and tobacco, faded after several year's service, the odd bottle of mineral water, jars of sweets, and buns and cakes under glass domes. The outside walls were decorated with enamel plates advertising Mazawattee Tea, Oxo, Seidlitz Powders, Quaker Oats, Holloway Pills, Hudson's Soap and Fry's

Cocoa, some of which the shop keeper had not stocked for many years. It never occurred to anyone to take the signs down since they gave colour to the surroundings.

The high class confectionery shops in the High Street, like Keene's, sold Cadbury's and Fry's chocolate, Macintosh's and Everton toffee and expensive boxes of chocolates, but there was also a great demand for home-made sweets which came from the small corner shops and itinerant vendors with their barrows. Boiled sweets in mint or lemon flavour competed with mint humbugs and gobstoppers. Parrot's sweet factory in Lagland Street made Poole rock in sticks six inches or twelve inches long, pink on the outside, with the name running through the whole length. Toffee was made in shallow tins and broken up by the shopkeeper with a small hammer. Other favourites of ours were sherbet dabs, licorice strips and bootlaces. In West Street, the Dorset Mineral Company bottled lemonade, cherryade, cream soda and lime juice and soda at a penny a bottle. We often broke the bottles to get the glass stoppers for marbles, and we could never understand how they were put there in the first place.

Some butchers killed their own meat and most of the animal was for sale, including bladders of lard, black puddings made from pig's blood, chitterlings, tripe, pigs' trotters and cheeks, as well as the usual prime cuts. My mother always favoured silverside which we bought from the High Street shop of Mr Bailey, a fat, genial butcher. He wore a blue and white striped apron and a straw boater which kept the dripping blood from his head. A sharpening steel was tied to his waist. The shop floor was covered with sawdust, spread by the errand boy when he arrived in the morning, and meat carcasses hung on steel hooks around the shop. Mr Bailey cut the joints, sawed bones and used a cleaver while the customer waited, and it was sometimes alleged that he weighed his thumb as well as the joint. Such pleasantries he dismissed with a grin: 'Is there anything else today? Lamb chops? A nice piece of steak? Thank you, see you next week.' At Christmas time, he and his fellow butchers excelled themselves by covering the whole of their shop fronts with turkeys, geese, chickens, hares and rabbits. They hung from the eaves to the pavement, leaving just enough room to get into the shop. The birds hung head downwards, plucked but not disembowelled or beheaded, and needed preparation by the purchaser. It was essential that the gall bladder was not broken, otherwise the Christmas dinner would be ruined. The hares and rabbits were harled but still in their skins. Shopkeepers encouraged people to subscribe to a Christmas club, collecting a few pence per week, the total to be spent at Christmas. On Christmas Eve, we walked round the streets to see the tinsel, Christmas trees and paper chains while the Poole Town Band and the Salvation Army

Butcher's shop.

played carols, moving from Topp's Corner to the Quay, rattling their collection boxes. Mother always made at least twenty four Christmas puddings which were boiled in the copper and lasted for many months.

Many shops would deliver goods, either by errand boys with large baskets on the handlebars of their bicycles, by hand-barrow, or by horse-drawn cart. Grocers from the High Street would send a man once a week to take orders which were delivered on an allotted day, but mother and I often went to the shop instead and waited while the order was made up. Items like flour, tea, sugar and dried peas were stored in drawers behind the counter, from which they were extracted with scoops to be weighed on brass scales. Biscuits were kept loose in square tins, and there were always broken biscuits for sale. One side of the shop sold butter and margarine which was cut from large blocks and patted into pounds or half pounds with two wooden patters, the grocer taking a small bit off or putting a bit on to get the correct weight. Cheese was cut into wedges with a steel wire. Ham, roast pork and cold beef were cut on a slicer while we waited, or we might get some Shippam's potted meat or bloater paste to eat with bread and butter as an alternative to jam. Salted codfish still came to Poole from Newfoundland as it had done for two hundred years. It had to be soaked in water for a very long time to get rid of all the salt. When the order was complete, the money was put into a cup on

Guildhall market.

an overhead wire and propelled by a spring loaded handle across the shop to the cash desk, the change coming back the same way.

Mother also joined the Co-operative Society where some of the profits were returned to the customers every six months. The shop was opposite the Round House and as I grew older I was sometimes entrusted with the Co-op card on which our purchases were recorded. On Thursdays, the ground floor of the Guildhall was opened as a market and Mr Mullins of Bloxworth sold fresh vegetables from his garden, pigeons for three pence and rabbits for six pence, which he brought the twelve miles by horse and cart. There were several local bakers, Baverstocks' in New Street, Granny Betts' in Thames Street and Mr Phillips' in Market Street, who baked their bread in stone ovens. Mr Phillips started baking at four o'clock in the morning and by breakfast time he would be leaving his Market Street premises with a handcart to start deliveries. We would buy doughcakes, buns, rolls and bread hot from the oven. The week before Easter, he came round to take orders for hot cross buns, which his sons delivered at six o'clock on Good Friday morning.

There were also itinerant traders like the Italian ice cream men with their highly painted barrows, topped with shades, who sold penny cones and two penny wafers in the summer, and roast chestnuts in the winter. Costermongers' barrows stood at strategic points in the High Street, selling fruit, vegetables and fish. On Saturday mornings we would be awakened by a man calling 'Young spring water cre-e-e-esses', or by the muffin man with his bell and a basket on his head. Another familiar cry was 'Any old rags and bo-o-ones?'.

Gypsies sold clothes pegs and bunches of violets from door to door and French onion men were regular visitors. Mr Dobell brought our milk in a large churn, fastened to a low-slung cart drawn by a pony. We would take a jug out to him in the street and he would ladle out a pint or half pint. Another caller was the postman who wore a cap with a peak front and back and always knocked after delivering the post. Once a week the coalman came round with his horse and flat dray, carrying a ton of coal in sacks. He wore a leather waistcoat and a sack over the back of his head to protect him from the weight of the coal. He sold whole or half hundredweights and carried them on his back to the coal-house. For those that could afford it he would deliver a ton and tip it into the cellar through the circular wooden or iron trapdoor in the pavement. I hated the laborious job of fetching coal up the stone steps of the cellar, which had to be done most days of the winter. Domestic help was cheap, however, and readily available. We had a succession of 'dailies', young girls who helped with the housework and probably earned not much more than the errand boys, five shillings a week with midday meal and tea provided.

Cobblers abounded in the town. All the boot and shoe shops repaired footwear and would fit rubber sole and heels, Blakey's Tips or hobnails to reinforce working boots. By 1914, shoes were replacing boots. Plastic was unheard of, but canvas-sided boots and plimsolls came into fashion, and mass produced footwear came to the town with company shops like Lilley and Skinner, Frisby's and Bata. These were in competition with local shops like J. A. Hawkes, which had been in business for a couple of generations. Small cobblers thrived in the side streets, and signs saying 'Boot repairs done here' appeared in many parlour windows, the work being done in a shed in the garden. These were the days of menial jobs. Sandwich men paraded the High Street with a board back and front advertising local shops. Road sweepers with brush and barrow cleaned the same street, year in year out. Chimney sweeping was an honourable profession but very hard work, pushing scrapers and brushes up chimneys, which always had a 'dog-leg' in them, for the princely sum of two and sixpence a time. The town's refuse was collected by men with horse and cart and taken to the tip at Baiter, the men wearing 'Gor Blimey' trousers with straps around them below the knee. They had large sacks hanging on the sides of the cart and one of their perks was to save jam jars which would be bought by Harman's in Fish Street at a half penny each.

Bill stickers travelled the town on bicycles with paste pot and brushes, plastering every vacant spot with advertisements, announcements of fetes, concerts and sporting events, putting bill on top of bill. In exasperation, a notice would be put up saying 'Bill stickers will be prosecuted', in reply to which some local wit would scrawl underneath 'Bill Stickers is innocent'. Householders were equally exasperated by a continual stream of door to door callers, beggars, tramps, tinkers and knife-grinders, while letter boxes were crammed with advertisements. Signs on doors and gates proclaimed 'No hawkers, no circulars' or 'Beware of the dog' (whether there was a dog or not).

The Poole fire engine was stored in King Street, a horse-drawn vehicle, manned by a volunteer brigade. The procedure was to take two horses from any garbage vehicle which was near to the station, and men, horses and engine were ready in a very short time. With the brass bell ringing, the engine turned into Market Street and then had a clear run to the 'Top of the Town' and over the level crossing, (that is if it was open), and on to the outskirts of the town where the horses could be given their heads. The most spectacular turn-out that I ever saw was in 1913 at Sandbanks. Here an almost permanent camping site had been established. Marquees, bell tents and pup tents were all in rather close proximity, and a child had knocked over an oil stove and set fire to a tent. A general conflagration seemed imminent. With plenty of sand available, however, the fire was extinguished, but someone had called the fire brigade from its station six miles away. The engine passed me in Sandbanks Road as I was cycling to the camp, nine men on board wearing brass helmets and axes hanging from their belts and the captain resplendent in a silver helmet. The men were seated three aside on the body of the engine, with the captain in front beside the driver who brandished a whip. Strapped to the rear of the vehicle was Tommy Phillips, all five feet of him, whose job it was to stoke the fire that raised the steam in the boiler to run the pumps. As they passed me on the straight, the men were being thrown around because of the uneven road, and were holding on to the leather straps, although they were no doubt also strapped in. The driver urged his charges to greater effort, but it was the horses who were the heroes of the day to a ten year old boy trying to keep up with them. Foaming at the mouth, their manes matted with sweat, they charged on. I caught them up on Lilliput Hill as they plodded upwards and then slowly descended the other side with a drag shoe on one of the rear wheels, but they passed me again on Shore Road. When they arrived at the camp, the fire was out and it only remained for Mr

Winter, the captain, to make his report.

These horses were the heavy draught animals who pulled the garbage trucks, brewery drays and timber yard vehicles. Their normal duties were a very leisurely business, entailing frequent stops, some of which lasted a long time. What induced them to drag a heavy vehicle with nine men on board at breakneck speed along a road that gave no resilience to their heavily-shod feet? Was this a throwback to their wild ancestors who thundered over hills and plains, never having seen iron shoes or harness? I thought that they were magnificent and for many years I decided that I wanted to be a fireman.

The products of Marston's Brewery in Market Street and Styring's Brewery in Towngate Street, with its two large cooling towers, were sold at the many public houses in the town. The *Vine*, the *Yeoman*, the *Angel* and the *Crown* encircled the Guildhall, and along the Quay was the *Portsmouth Hoy*, the *Jolly Sailor*, the *Poole Arms*, its facade covered with green faience from Carter's pottery, the *King Charles* in Thames Street and the *Rising Sun* in Fish Street, all of which served the sailors and dockers. The *Antelope* and the *London Hotel* in High Street were old coaching inns. The *Bull's Head*, the *White Hart*, the *King's Head* and the *Ansty Arms* at the top of town competed with the *Railway Tavern* in East Street and the *Railway Hotel* and the *Queen Charlotte* in

Poole Fire Brigade.

39

Towngate Street. They all had their private bars which were exclusive to the properly dressed, and public bars for those who were not so high on the social ladder. Through a side entrance was the bottle and jug department for home drinkers, and it was a common sight to see people taking a jug for their midday or evening beer 'straight from the wood'. Because of the bottle and jug, drinking was largely a social habit, and drunkenness, if any, usually occurred on Saturday nights. Sometimes a drunk would be taken to the Market Street police station roped to one of Harman's hand trucks, pushed by two policemen, and this could result in ten days in Dorchester prison. Well-meaning citizens would meet the train when he arrived back at Poole station, to try to put him back on the straight and narrow path.

In the early twenties, a number of people, chiefly members of the Adult School, were concerned about the welfare of the inmates of our prisons. One such gentleman organised a concert in which I was involved, for the men in Dorchester gaol. It was a very interesting experience. Our party consisted of the usual tenors, sopranos and basses, accompanied by violin, cello and piano. About one hundred men were already seated when we entered the hall. The Governor welcomed us and, facing the audience, I recognised about half a dozen Poole worthies sitting in the back row who clapped enthusiastically as they obviously recognised us. They all seemed very happy and sang the choruses of the popular songs, but things got a little out of hand when they were asked what they would like to end the concert. The response was deafening; everyone shouted at once, the Poole contingent louder than any. The Governor stood up and demanded silence. 'We will not sing 'I'll See You Again'', he asserted, and nearly brought the house down. Even the warders smiled. 'We'll sing 'Ten Green Bottles'', (which was about the extent of their singing ability). I doubt if the prison had ever heard so much noise and we were cheered out of the hall. The organiser said that he had never heard anything like it.

CHAPTER FOUR

The trams were a cheap form of transport from Poole station to Bournemouth Square which we used for weekend family outings. At Bournemouth, we walked along the promenade or the pier and through the gardens where we could sail model boats in the River Bourne. The trams went by way of Brown Bottom or Park Gates East, as it later became known, where the line divided, one route running up the hill, via North Road to Sea View, and the other continuing through Lower Parkstone until the lines met up again near Branksome Station. At holiday time the trams were usually overcrowded and the conductor had to be very firm with his exhortations. 'Pass right down the car please. Full up on top. No standing on the platform' Then he would put his arm across the entrance to prevent any more passengers getting on, (which was awkward if some of the family had been left behind), and ring the bell, or if he was on the top deck, blow his whistle. Energetic young men would run after the tram and sometimes the conductor would grab them as the driver increased speed and drag them on board. On other occasions he would show his disinterest by turning his back and going up the stairs. The conductor often found it difficult to push his way through to the front of the crowded tram, taking money, giving change and punching tickets, and by the time he arrived back at the platform, some of the upstairs passengers had got off without paying. Some conductors would just stand on the platform taking the money. As the tram slowed he would shout: 'Wait till the tram stops' and 'Serve you right', to anyone who did not wait and fell into the road.

There was a problem when it rained because the top deck was open and everybody wanted to go inside. Quite frequently the traffic was disrupted because the electric arm came off the overhead wire and the conductor had to take a long bamboo pole to put it back again. Once a tram lost control at the top of Poole Hill, raced down to the Triangle, rounded the corner at Robson's, and plunged into Bournemouth Gardens, lying upturned by the side of the Bourne Stream. Seven people were killed and twenty six injured.

As an alternative to the trams, we sometimes went to Bournemouth by train, but Bournemouth West station was a long

Near Park Gates, Poole.

way from the Square and Bournemouth Central even further. In each case we had to catch a tram which was by then probably full. Nevertheless we liked the trains, the engine driver and fireman looking on as passengers climbed aboard and the wheel-tapper banging the wheels with his hammer. I always hoped that he would find a cracked one, but he never did. The porters shouted 'Mind the doors', and slammed them shut, while the guard blew his whistle and waved his green flag for the train to start, jumping into the van as the train moved off. At Bournemouth West station, which was a terminus, I always looked to see how near the engine was to the buffers, because once the driver had failed to stop, and the engine mounted the platform and finished up in the waiting room. Waiting for trains was rather tedious because the waiting rooms were hardly luxurious. They smelt of smoke and the benches were covered with a shiny black material. The lighting was a flickering gas jet and the heating came from a cast iron fireplace on to which a porter occasionally threw a shovelful of dusty coal.

Poole railway station had penny-in-the-slot machines dispensing Fry's chocolate. One day when I inserted my penny, the machine continued to deliver chocolate every time I pulled the tray. I collected four bars, but was so frightened that I ran away and dared not go back for more, having visions of Bobby Blues taking me off to the police station. The station also had huge cast iron weighing machines, but platform tickets were many years away. As the train came in, the head porter would shout all the stops to Waterloo (for the London and

High Street level crossing.

South Western Railway), or to Blandford and Bath for the Somerset and Dorset line, known locally as the slow and doubtful. Outside, porters waited with their handcarts to take luggage to the hotels for a modest fee. The traveller caught on the wrong side of the closed gates was faced with running over the bridge, waiting for the gates to open or dodging through the wicket gate and across the line, which was illegal, not to say dangerous.

Originally the railway had come to Poole from Wimborne, with the station at Hamworthy, and when a station was proposed for Poole, it was agreed that every train would stop there in exchange for two level crossings, one in Towngate Street and one in High Street. It saved the railway company the cost of bridges and a high level station, but the crossings were a source of constant frustration for nearly one hundred years. The gates in the High Street were operated from a signal box, and those at the station, by hand. As the speed of motor cars increased, it needed considerable skill to operate the gates, as the railway man, Andy Hodge, had to decide when to let a car through, allowing time to walk from his cabin, lift the bolts and pull the gates across. During my sixty one years in Poole I never heard of a car hitting either set of gates. A popular refrain, sung to the tune of 'A Little Bit of Heaven' went: 'They built two level crossings just to make the people swear, / And built a few gasometers to purify the air, / And they dotted it with coal dust to make us wash our hair, / And they called it Puddle Poole'.

Because of the use of horses for transport, Poole was well

supplied with corn merchants. Importers and wholesalers like Yeatman's, Christopher Hill and Dorset Farmers operated on the Quay and retailers such as Mr Stevens, Mr Schofield and Mr Dean had shops in the High Street. At the corner of New Street and High Street, Mr Christopher ran a saddler's shop, where he repaired horse harness and nose bags, and sold curry combs and brushes for horse grooming. Horse troughs were placed in convenient locations so that horses could slake their thirst. There was one in Paradise Street made of hollowed out Purbeck stone, one at the foot of North Road, and one in Lower Parkstone. There was also a pound for straying animals in Pound Street and one on the corner of Pound Lane and Fernside Road which was still there in the 1920's. Mr Swain, the town's blacksmith, had a forge near to the George Hotel and I was often late for school because I stopped to watch him shoe a horse. The forge was open to the street, and huge cart horses, gentlemen's riding horses and children's ponies were all shod in full view of the passers-by. The bellows were pumped by hand, the red hot shoe burning the hoof gave off a glorious smell as it was fitted, and the hissing as it was dropped into the can of water was irresistible. I was always scared that he would put a nail into the soft part of the horse's foot, but I never saw it happen. Mr Swain also 'shot' iron hoops on to the wheels of farm carts. These were hammered red hot on to the wheel and then cooled and shrunk by the application of buckets of water which sent clouds of steam spreading out into the street. He would also make us iron hoops and hooks with which to 'troll' them.

As the use of motor cars and trucks developed, the maintenance of roads became a problem. Before the advent of tarmacadam, water carts drawn by horses sprayed the roads to lay the dust. The High Street, from the Wesleyan Chapel to the Round House, was laid with wooden blocks set in tar. These were about the size of a brick and about half an inch thick, and they lasted well until work had to be done to gas and water mains, when it became difficult to replace them. Eventually they were taken up and the road covered with tarmacadam. The Model T Ford came to Poole before the first World War, and the first public transport from Poole to Sandbanks was operated by a fleet of them, running from Park Gates East to the Haven. The fare was sixpence each way and a car could take four passengers with only a canvas hood protecting them from the weather. The cars were privately owned and there was a great deal of touting for custom. We preferred to cycle to Sandbanks by way of the Bunny and Whitecliff, as a shilling was a considerable sum to outlay. Travelling by Harvey's boat from the Quay was also much more enjoyable. Many people rode bicycle, normally upright roadsters which were often second hand. Mr Rice, a bearded gentleman who

Motor Park, Sandbanks. 192.

wore a tall round hat, used to ride a penny-farthing bicycle from Heckford Park, which he mounted from a 'stepper' attached to the small back wheel. Mr Holmes, who owned a temperance hotel opposite Topp's Corner, rode a tricycle around the town.

The town had plenty of characters. There was Mr Stevens, the corn merchant, who always said as he dispensed chaff for the horses: 'Come on, my boy. Don't you know how to hold up a sack properly?', and demonstrated how it should be done. He used to sell besoms made of heather twigs for nine pence each, wire netting, maize, bird seed, potatoes and artificial fertiliser. Mr Dean's shop was at the tram terminus and he too was a corn merchant. In his later years he would sit in an armchair and always had time to talk to any small boy who stopped by. Alderman Harry Cole was a genial old gentleman, known and liked by everyone. Bearded and wearing a long frock coat, he would doff his top hat to all and sundry. With his sons he ran a furniture shop and was the town's undertaker. Whenever I met him I would say, 'Good morning, Mr Cole', and he always doffed his hat and said, 'Good morning, my boy. Nice weather for the time of year'. He was a great supporter of the rights of the poor and could be relied upon to raise matters that affected them whenever the Council met. A constant stream of people came to his shop needing help and advice, and on public occasions there was always someone who shouted 'Good old Harry' and meant it.

Mr Buckle in Market Street mended umbrellas, a trade which has completely disappeared, as today people just throw them away and buy another. He also put brass tips on walking sticks and sold parasols. Mr Cole, the jeweller provided the High Street with the correct time by his drum clock, and was also the time keeper for all the athletic sports in the park. Some said that it was because he was the only man in Poole who owned a stop watch. Alderman Dolph Shutler sold seamen's clothing and although he was never known to play any sport, he was a great supporter of football clubs, cricket teams and the Poole rowing club, becoming secretary of most of them. He was a keen collector of team photographs which he gladly and proudly showed to me whenever I entered his shop. The best of these was a shot of the local team, the players facing the camera, arms folded, the ball and trophies proudly displayed and the goalkeeper in the middle of the back row, facing sideways because he thought that he looked better in profile.

Mrs Dinevan had a small shop in New Orchard and in the winter months sold hot peppermint, sasparilla, blackcurrant and lemon drinks at a penny a glass. She also had a machine which gave electric shocks for a penny in the slot, and she would creep up behind the operator and pour water over his hands to increase the sensation. Tom Hockey was a well-liked, vociferous costermonger whose barrow was always placed outside the Wesleyan Church, while his voice could be heard from Topp's Corner to the Post Office. In the summer he used to shout 'Fresh mackerel', (but it sounded like 'macro'), 'Fish-o. Three for a shilling', until the policeman told him to keep his voice down, at which he was inclined to argue, making more noise than ever. The ironmongers, corn merchants and small shopkeepers used to put a great deal of their stock on the pavement under a sun blind which rolled up over the shop window. Once, an enterprising customer picked up a garden fork from Boone and Giblett's, took it into the shop and asked for his money back, because 'Father said it was too big'. He was paid the money, but later they caught him and he ended up in the Police Court.

Harry White, the phrenologist, lived in West Street. He was baldheaded with long wispy hair at the back and did not give the impression of being very affluent, but he was very knowledgeable about his subject and the ways of the world. In his parlour window he displayed a drawing of a human head divided by thick lines into areas denoting kindness, intelligence, patience and also some of the less desirable attributes. He would 'tell your bumps' for a modest sum, but I think that we were too scared to take advantage of his talents. Many years later he lectured to the Adult School one Sunday morning, selecting two young lads as subjects. He pointed to various parts of their heads and we were convinced at the time that we could see the difference in their characters visible in the shape of their heads. As a boy, I felt that a reading would be useful only if his diagnosis were favourable.

A very different sort of attraction was Mr Stokes, the Town Crier who walked the town in a long blue cloak and cocked hat, both decorated with braid. He would ring his bell and shout: 'O Yea, O Yea, O Yea' but I was never very impressed with his announcements because they seemed to be for very trivial occasions, unworthy of his dignified appearance. However he made up for this when he performed his official duties as mace bearer. When the mayor had been chosen by the Council, a procession was held on the next Sunday morning from the Guildhall to St. James' church. All the civic dignitaries, councillors and aldermen in cocked hats and cloaks, the legal fraternity in wigs and gowns, took their places behind the Poole town band. The boy scouts (of whom I was one), the girl guides, the boys' brigade and the fire brigade all followed, rather out of step. It was more of a Sunday morning stroll than a march and the only group keeping time was the band. The rector conducted the service, with all the important people in the body of the church while we lesser mortals took our seats in the gallery where scout hats and poles were something of a problem. The town mace, magnificent in shining gold - or was it brass? - was carried with great aplomb and dignity on the shoulder of Mr Stokes, marching in front of the Mayor and wearing his hat fore and aft in the tradition of Wellington. Apart from the Mayor, in a red cloak and mayoral chain, he was by far the most impressive member of the gathering. To me the mace was of great importance, surely as great as the one of which Cromwell said: 'Take away that bauble'. The procession also included the 5th Poole scouts which had gradually established its own brass and bugle band. We played such songs as 'Marching through Georgia', with Phillips, our cornet player, and six bugles. Eventually it developed into a full brass band, but I gave up around 1919 as I had by then grown to nearly six feet tall, and marching behind a band in shorts with a pole was just too much.

Politically, Britain was divided at the time into two parties, Tories and Liberals. Mr Van Raalte, who owned Brownsea Island, contested East Dorset for the Tory Party, but Poole was strongly Liberal and he was defeated by Freddy Guest, the younger brother of Lord Wimborne of Canford. Together with his wife, Lady Cornelia, Lord Wimborne was a great benefactor to the town. The Wimborne family gave the Cornelia Hospital in Longfleet Road, the Library near the Quay, and the land which formed Poole Park, and supported the welfare of the inhabitants. Freddy Guest held the seat of East Dorset for many years, defeating Col. Nicholson in one pre-war election. Eventually, however, he was unseated on a charge of bribery because one of his relations, Lord Rodney, had hired motor vehicles to take voters to the polls. The election was held again and his brother, Major Guest, stood against Nicholson. We Liberals sang 'Hey, hey, clear the way. Here comes the galloping major', and tried to wreck the Tory meetings by shouting 'Cuckoo' whenever Nicholson tried to speak. It was all great fun. The Liberal colour was red, and the Tory, blue, and my father hung a large red flag from the bedroom window until someone threatened to throw a brick through it and he took it down.

It was considered a great merit to sing ribald songs about the other side, and rhymsters composed lyrics to the tunes of well-known songs: 'We'll hang Van Raalte from a sour apple tree', to the tune of 'John Brown's Body' and 'Poor old Cuckoo wants a nest' aimed at Nicholson. The result of the election was proclaimed by the Returning Officer from the balcony of the Guildhall above the curved steps. The winner always stood on his right hand side and we cheered as they appeared because it was always Freddy Guest or his party. On this occasion the Liberals were so sure that Major Guest would win, that they had organised a torch light procession with torches made out of sacking, soaked with tar fastened to long poles. My father made a dozen. Fortunately, the Major won by an even larger majority. His supporters attached ropes to his carriage and pulled it round the town, singing the Major's theme song.

The first Labour candidate to contest East Dorset was named Smith, and he was beaten but received over 1000 votes. From the balcony of the Guildhall he declared that he was satisfied with the result and was certain that five years earlier, he would not have received a hundred. His supporters in the crowd cheered and Freddy did not look too pleased because his majority was well down on the previous election. Judith Hart who later became a Labour minister under Harold Wilson, also contested East Dorset in her first attempt at election. After Hall Caine, Poole sent its own representative to Parliament, and a Poole man, Alex Glassey, held it for the Liberals for a term. Then Mervyn Wheatley, also from Poole, was elected as a Conservative member, and to date no Labour candidate has succeeded in the seat.

Suffragettes were also active in Poole, shouting 'Votes for women' at political meetings. I once saw them thrown out of the Amity Hall, and on my way to school one morning, saw a post-box on Longfleet Road dripping with tar. My mother once went to a women's meeting in Bournemouth, thinking that it was to do with the Co-operative Society, and arrived home rather shaken. An enthusiastic suffragette had tried to recruit her into the movement with instructions about

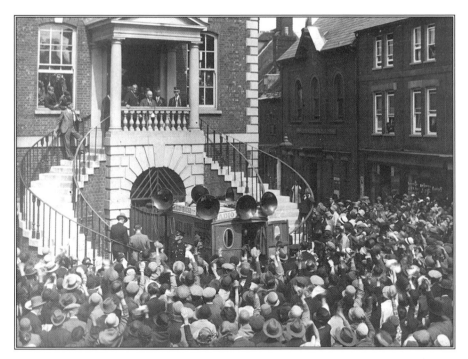

The election of Alex Glassey, 1929.

how to throw a brick through a shop window, an operation which was for her completely beyond the bounds of possibility. She could hardly lift a brick, let alone throw it, and I am sure that she had no great wish to have the vote.

The local Petty Sessions were held in the Guildhall, and in my late teens I sometimes stood at the back of the hall to listen to the trials of local miscreants. Serious cases of stealing, assault, arson and similar misdemeanours were referred to the court by the local magistrates, juries were empanelled, and the judge on the Western Circuit presided. One case I remember was of a local fowl stealer who came regularly before the court. The first time I heard a charge against him, the evidence was that a local farmer had lost turkeys and fowls a week before Christmas. The police had no doubt about the offender; he had been convicted several times before for the same offence. Arrested, he strenuously denied any knowledge of the birds, but the loft of his house was found to be full of feathers. Towards the end of the hearing he was asked if he had anything to say and he complained that he had not had legal assistance. The judge looked over his glasses and suggested that the accused was quite capable of defending himself (implying that he had had a lot of practice). Continuing his speech, the defendant proclaimed 'Ladies and gentlemen of the jury, You are here as Britishers to do your duty', which brought laughter from the back of the court. The usher shouted 'Silence in court' and a policeman moved nearer to the spectators. The prisoner denied everything, he was not lying, he never had, (but he did not mention the feathers). Under cross-examination he was asked: 'Do you always tell the truth in court?' 'Yes'. 'You did not tell the truth last year when you were sentenced to twelve months'. 'I did, but the jury did not believe me'. They did not believe him this time, and he was duly found guilty. I later served on several juries and heard of a paternity case, the burning of a hayrick, armed assault and the mugging of an old lady by the fowl stealer.

As the boundaries of the town enclosed more areas, the cases were held in the Municipal Buildings and the Guildhall became neglected. The building had been given to the town by its two Members of Parliament in the days of pocket boroughs, and had witnessed dramas in court, the counting of votes, social functions and the deliberations of the Town Council. Its ground floor had been a market and had housed the municipal baths. On its eastern side was a bullet hole, the aftermath of a murder, which could be seen about ten feet from the north east corner. Eventually, netting was put across the gates at the bottom of the curved steps and the archway between them was bricked up and painted. The two crystal chandeliers which once graced the ceiling of the main hall disappeared and in spite of enquiries by Alderman Cole, were never found. The building entered a new phase as a museum.

CHAPTER FIVE

I have been told that my camping life began when I was one year old. The Boer War had ended twelve months before I was born and war surplus items came on the market, probably for the first time in history. My father bought a bell tent for thirty shillings from Messrs Gasson of Rye, complete with free oil lamp and a gadget with four hooks which could be fastened to the tent pole. It was decided to camp among the pines at Sandbanks. My mother and father were in their early twenties and did not know much about camping. The first problem was to put up the tent. After putting three guy-ropes on the cap of the tent, they pushed the pole upright and mother held it while father hammered in three pegs in roughly the right position. Having managed to get the whole thing reasonably straight, they then put inside, believe it or not, a double bedstead with pillows and a feather bed, two armchairs, a sofa, a wash stand and a chest of drawers. It must have been a fair sized load for a pony and cart, their only form of transport. As an extra precaution they put out a few more lines. At about ten o'clock, they went to bed, with me presumably in a cot. At one o'clock in the morning, they were awakened by a violent shaking of the tent and father rushed to prevent it falling over. There was a lot of swearing outside and a voice said 'What a bloody stupid place to put a tent'. One guy-line had been stretched across the footpath used by the coast guards to get to their lookout at the harbour mouth and one of them coming home after a spell of duty had tripped over it.

However, this did not deter my parents. They became pioneers of camping at Sandbanks and camped for the next ten years until Mr Meaby, the Canford agent, disposed of the land in the 1920's. Before the first world war, the Sandbanks peninsula was covered in pine trees and there were very few buildings apart from the Haven Hotel, James Harvey's house and business premises, and a few sheds for boats which operated on the harbour side. Building began on the Channel side, and when Lord Wimborne decided to sell the land, the high ground was gradually developed. One of the first houses to be built was on a sand hill called High Horse Manger. The general opinion was that it would not last but go the same way as Simpson's Folly, but it was still there thirty years later. Other sand hills were built on, and with the making of Panorama Road, the land on the harbour side was developed rapidly, while the pine trees were decimated. There were no tree preservation orders, and the houses built between Shore Road and the council chalets destroyed a veritable forest. Blown sand then became a problem, with stone walls and fences taking the place of trees. In contrast, Canford Cliffs and Branksome Park retained a large number of their trees, as the houses were larger and their grounds more spacious. Here the ground was more stable and the trees themselves larger, part of the plantation which had given Bournemouth the reputation of a health resort. The aroma of the pine trees and their resin was considered to be very healthy and of benefit to people with consumption.

There had always been a ferry from the Haven to Shell Bay since the days of Elizabeth I, and my earliest recollection of it, in about 1908, was of a rowing boat, propelled by two men. It was a difficult passage, three hundred yards wide, with almost impossible currents to contend with on the full flood or ebb tide. Mr Poulain, a Frenchman who owned the Haven Hotel, introduced a motor boat with a special bow for landing on the beach and built an iron pier on the Sandbanks side. His boat was run by Scottie. Eventually, after he sold the hotel, Harvey's ran several boats from small wooden landing stages. They were joined by Tommy Davis, and ferrying became big business, with touts importuning people along Sandbanks Road. Complications arose when the chain ferry was introduced in the 1920's, and there was a dispute as to whether the ferry had a monopoly in its charter. The case went to the High Court and the company lost, to the satisfaction

Camping at Sandbanks.

Sandbanks Ferry.

Banks Road, Sandbanks.

of the public whose sympathy was with the small boats.

From about 1910, Poole Corporation allowed wooden beach huts to be erected on the 'rough side' at Sandbanks. They also provided communal huts where people could change for bathing. Both men's and women's costumes covered the body from knee to neck, and the women's were embellished with skirts, flounces and mob caps. Changing on the beach for adults was unheard of, but as we had to pay to use the huts, we youngsters always went along Shore Road a mile towards Bournemouth and changed by the sea wall. One

Saturday afternoon, four of us, the oldest being twelve, were sitting on the beach well back from the sea at Simpson's Folly when a policeman appeared. He had seen us changing from about fifty yards away, propped his bicycle against the wall and walked along the beach to tackle us. 'WHAT do you think you are doing?' he demanded. Scared stiff I replied 'Changing'. 'You can't do that here. Supposing some ladies came along? If I catch you again I'll take you to the police station'. I had no answer to that although in fact there was no-one in sight and the beach was clear of people for several miles. We all dressed quickly and sat there until he had gone back to his bicycle, not daring to change again in case he returned and found us in the water. This policeman was stationed at Parkstone and cycled regularly to Sandbanks, wearing bicycle clips on his trousers. For the rest of the summer we kept a look-out for him and hid until he had passed, swimming and changing on the beach a mile or so nearer to Bournemouth, because we reckoned that it was unlikely he would walk that far along the sand in full uniform.

My grandfather Gale was a shoemaker by trade and very skilled with his hands. In 1911, he bought an old lifeboat that came from an ocean liner and had it placed in the yard where my father kept the horses. Here he converted it into a houseboat, building a square cabin with an open front deck and cockpit. It had two windows on each side, for which my mother made some brightly coloured curtains, and there were stout hessian hammocks for beds. These stretched the width of the cabin and were removed in the daytime, giving a large room with settees on both sides. A short ladder hung over the stern. Several facetious suggestions were made for a name, but the old boy had already made up his mind that it would be 'St. Crispin', the patron saint of shoemakers. At eight years old, I thought that this was brilliant.

The great day for launching arrived. The vessel had to be taken from the yard to Harvey's slipway about half a mile away on the west shore of Poole harbour. My grandfather had borrowed a huge flat trolley with iron wheels, and the houseboat was jacked up on to it and fastened down with ropes. About twenty local youngsters were recruited and ropes were tied to the front bearers of the trolley. At the word of command, everyone pulled, and the flat iron wheels moved slowly down the yard. There was an archway leading to the street which had been measured carefully before building commenced, but unfortunately my father had built up the roadway, and the roof of the houseboat would not pass under. Spades were brought, the road was dug away, and St. Crispin just scraped her way into the street. The procession caused a great deal of interest as it passed along Market Street into King Street, round the corner into

West Street and then on to West Shore. Two stout eighteen year olds took charge and shouted instructions. People came out of their houses to encourage the boys to greater effort. Steering was a problem. The two front wheels could swivel for the corners but because of the weight, they had to be manhandled. Fortunately, there was no traffic since the motor car was a very rare visitor to these back streets of Poole. We reached the slipway safely and the floating home was reversed and pushed gently down the slope, when at the eleventh hour the whole operation came near to disaster. The slipway was slippery with seaweed and although the rope-handlers dug in their heels, they lost control and the trolley began to gather speed. The ropes were abandoned and *St. Crispin* hit the water sending up a bow wave that would have done justice to the *Titanic*. Slipping off the trolley, she keeled over to about forty degrees and grandfather admitted afterwards that he thought she had gone. Slowly, however, she righted herself, her brass name plate gradually assumed a horizontal position, and she was safely tied up to the quay. Largess was handed out to the hauliers and they adjourned to a nearby sweet shop.

The next day we made our way to the wharf and loaded bedding, food and our personal things. Mother was not at all happy about the proceedings because sleeping afloat was not her idea of holiday happiness. She refused to embark on the maiden voyage and chose instead to ride her bicycle the five miles to Sandbanks, her dress, which nearly touched the ground, with the mandatory small lead discs sewn into the hem, so that her legs would not show as she pedalled.

Charlie Harvey brought alongside his steam driven boat, the 'Pioneer', with its brass funnel newly polished with Brasso, and tossed us a towline. Grandfather called 'Cast off', and we were away, passing under Poole Bridge at two or three knots, turning to port at Stakes Buoy and travelling down the main channel until we reached Half Way Diver, which is a channel for small craft and fishing boats. We turned into Stoke's Lake to our prepared moorings which consisted of a traction engine wheel bought from Henry Burden who owned several such vehicles. The spot was marked with a bright red buoy which I grabbed with a boathook as the houseboat came to a stop and rolled gently on the placid water. Charlie Harvey having left, and mother having arrived with her bicycle, we rowed ashore in the dinghy we had towed astern, and helped her aboard, gingerly climbing the ladder on the stern of the houseboat. Meanwhile, grandfather returned to Poole on her bicycle.

My small brother and I spent a wonderful weekend fishing from the roof of the houseboat while mother fussed around, still nervous of the whole adventure. We went cockling and winkling, practised our rowing, one oar each, and on Tuesday morning, rowed father ashore so that he could cycle back to work. Mother sat in the stern, grimly grasping the edge of the boat as we rowed back to the houseboat. Feeling very confident, as we had been practising all the weekend, we urged mother to take hold of the ladder. She stood up, but when she grasped the top rung, her weight pushed the boat away so that she was faced with the choice of falling head first or feet first into the water. She chose the latter, but managed to drag herself over the stern, her voluminous skirt with the lead washers in it, hanging bedraggled around her ankles.

The next day she decided that this was the end of houseboats for her. She had spent a restless night because of the gentle lapping of the waves and the accompanying creak of the anchor chain. She was also certain that we had been going round in circles all night and had lost confidence in the traction engine wheel. After all, as she said, 'Wheels are meant to go round. We need a proper anchor'. Certainly we were facing the other way in the morning from the night before, but that was because the tide had turned. That evening father moved the ladder to the side of the cockpit and we practised rowing alongside. As mother grasped the ladder, we learned to hold on to the side of the houseboat.

House boats at Stoke's Lake

In time, mother largely lost her fear, and many happy years followed. We rowed and sailed in the safe channel of Stoke's Lake, ventured further into the deep water of the harbour, and fished off Bell Buoy in front of Brownsea Island or from the stakes marking the main channel. Grandfather bought another dinghy which he used to row the four miles to Sandbanks on the ebb tide on Sunday mornings, returning to Poole on the flood tide in the evenings. One fateful day, he miscalculated and he, my father and I started back rather late to find that the tide was already ebbing. We reached Half Way Diver and picked up the marker stakes, but then we found that the rowlock my father was using was loose in its hole, and if he put too much weight on it, he landed on his back in the bottom of the boat. This caused us to lose sight of the stakes and we found ourselves in the main channel where the markers were made from the trunks of large pine trees, rising about ten feet out of the water. It was a very dark night with no moon, but we knew that if we could follow the poles, we would reach the main Quay. Seated in the stern, I was the only one facing them and had to call out 'One coming up', as we slowly edged towards safety. We finally sighted the breakwater which protected the fishing fleet at about ten o'clock, having been expected back at seven thirty. Mother was anxiously pacing the fishermen's dock. She had told the men that we were late and there was talk of launching the lifeboat or at least a fishing boat, to look for us. After this, she was even less impressed with houseboats, rowing boats, and a family that still messed about in the awkward things.

In 1914, we saw the outbreak of war from the houseboat, having cycled to Sandbanks to pump out the bilges (a nasty job, particularly in winter). We saw a squad of coast guards, eight of them with a petty officer in charge, marching towards Lilliput Hill in single file on their way to war. They were reservists and we knew them personally as we had played with their children for the last four years.

In midwinter 1916, Poole experienced a hurricane and the houseboat foundered. Grandfather had her pulled ashore and sold her for thirty shillings because she had a hole in her side, having sunk on to the traction engine wheel. He unscrewed her name plate and we kept it for many years, a nostalgic memory of an adventurous period. He later built wooden huts on land rented from Lord Wimborne at ten shillings a year and we lived out some glorious summers there until about 1920, when my father was offered the land, (at least an acre), for £50. He did not buy it and today, of course, it would be priceless. So ended our association with Sandbanks which had lasted for over twenty years.

I was an enthusiastic member of the 5th Poole Boy Scouts group and enjoyed scouting. On one occasion Bill Tydeman and Dr Ewart

Hawkes, straight from the trenches in Flanders, took ten of us with a trek cart for a week in the New Forest. After catching the train to Brockenhurst we set off, pulling the cart, and finally ended up at Ringwood where we caught the train back to Poole. We camped among the ponies, swam in the rivers and cooked over a wood fire, singing songs around the fire in the evening, 'Ten Green Bottles', 'The Mermaid', 'The Battle Cry of Freedom' , and 'All through the Night'. In 1918, the Dorset Scouts' Association held a rally in Dorchester and the troops assembled at Maiden Castle to be inspected by Baden-Powell. The 5th Poole marched behind its brass band which had become the main reason for its existence. We lined up for inspection and the great man commented that some of us were not carrying poles. The Rev. Morley Worsam, our scout master, explained to B-P that the band, which was a long way down the line, belonged to us. I thought that we looked rather a motley collection and, at fifteen, felt a little ashamed.

As I grew older, scout uniform was hardly good enough. It was made of the cheapest materials and the hat became a disreputable thing after a few months in the rain, while the pole seemed to be pretty useless. Very much later, the movement discarded the hat and the pole, and eventually Rover Scouts went into slacks and berets. When B-P became Lord Baden-Powell of Gilwell, senior selected scouts were invited there annually to special rallies. I was sorry that I missed them, but by then I had more important interests. Nevertheless, scouting taught me a great deal from a love of the open air and nature, to tying knots or first aid which has often helped me in an emergency.

CHAPTER SIX

The Poole Carnival was held every year in August and Mr Cutler of Morton's Boots was the secretary and organiser. There was a carnival queen with attendants, a carnival coach, floats, some manned by the senior football clubs complete with trophies, and the Poole Rowing Club in red and white striped vests, the crew with oars and the cox with a rudder. They too displayed trophies won all along the South coast and round the Isle of Wight. There were prizes for the most decorative floats, motor cycles and side cars, decorated bicycles and commercial exhibits, as well as fancy dress prizes for adults and children. I remember one float with a caricature farm labourer in a smock and felt hat with a straw in his mouth, sitting in a wooden stocks with his legs outstretched. He wore a pair of new hobnailed boots and the slogan was 'Go Well-shod in Morton's Boots'. The procession lined up on the Quay and walked the length of the High Street to Brown Bottom, where it entered the Park and completed a

The Regent Theatre's Carnival float.

circuit of the track. The Poole Town Band led the way with the Branksome Band taking up a middle position. Once, the 5th Poole's single cornet, six bugles and two drums managed to get in on the act.

When the war came, a number of processions were organised to coincide with sports days in aid of the Red Cross. At one of them a Cambrai type tank came from Bovington and climbed over a huge pile of wood to demonstrate its prowess. There are three laps to the mile round the Park track, and mile races or relays were the main attraction. Long distance races finished with one lap round the track. Percy Hodge, the Olympic steeplechase champion, once ran in Poole in a mile handicap, and won easily after giving some entrants half a lap start.

The local Scouts' Association also ran its annual sports day in the Park and this included the half mile, the mile relay and a long distance race from the cricket pavilion, the length of the Park, through Seldown, round the Bunny and then once round the track. Harry Matthews of the 5th Poole usually won this event, and even I once won my half lap in the relay race, but in spite of this most unusual happening, we lost the race. Poole had always been strong in cycle racing. At the turn of the century, Steve Burge, a member of the Poole Cycling Club, was English champion, and in the early '30's the Poole Wheelers carried on the tradition. Bill Harvell came to Poole and led the Wheelers team to victory in the British Team Pursuit Championship, and cycle meetings were held on the Park track where he beat the English champion, Len Southall. The Wheelers later used the Poole Stadium which had a banked track, constructed on the site of the town's refuse tip by Mr Gallagher, the Poole Town Engineer.

Twice a year, a fair was held on the Ladies' Walking Field, which was so named because the women who worked in the rope factory there used to walk with the ropes as they came from the machines. The fairs were always held in the first week of May and the first week of November, and gave us a chance to indulge in the roundabouts, swings and hoopla, see the Fat Lady and the two-headed calf, and eat gingerbread, hokey-pokey, nougat and toffee apples. The Bartletts of Strand Street had a coconut shy which advertised nuts from their own plantations, while the whole show was run by Jacob Studt, who must have been a wealthy man. The barkers yelled themselves hoarse: 'Roll up, roll up. The greatest show on earth', and some of the side shows had a big drummer who tried to drown the cries of his neighbours with loud drumming, supplemented with bursts on a bugle.

Power and lighting were provided by huge traction engines which also supplied steam for the organ of the horse roundabout which could be heard a mile or so away. The strident notes of the organ, accompanied by drums, bells and whistles, shrieked out as the leaping horses rose and fell, some with two riders, some with one. Hundreds of light bulbs illuminated the huge machine and its traction engine, by far the most attractive draw in the show. Naphtha flares were used on the other attractions, especially the coconut shies. The boxing booth usually found a good audience as there was always a local battler willing to try his luck. It was said that the great Joe Beckett, heavyweight champion of England, started his career with Jacob Studt's fair.

I was fascinated by a man selling cough mixture. He had a loud, strong voice which he said came from taking his magic elixir once a day, and he offered to prove that its affect was instantaneous: 'I will show you, ladies and gentlemen, the wonderful effect my cough mixture has on a sore throat, and if there is any gentleman here who has...' and before he could finish, a hoarse voice said 'I have'. Everybody laughed and the salesman said, 'Come forward, sir. How long have you had a sore throat?' 'Three days', said the man in an almost inaudible voice. 'You should have come to see me before this, sir. Drink this'. The man took a swig from the bottle, pulled a face to show how strong the mixture was, swallowed, coughed, pulled another face and yelled 'I'm cured' at the top of his voice. Then they

Poole fair in 1958.

61

shook hands and the showman started to shout 'Roll up, roll up. One shilling a bottle. The greatest cure on earth'. I was astonished, but some people did buy a bottle and I decided that they must be his friends and relations. However the next evening he was still there and different people were buying. I think that he was just a comedian doing it for fun. Towards the end of the fair, I saw him selling Medicinal Compound, an American cure-all, and doing a roaring trade.

Once I was caught out by a swindler who had two turned poles, about two feet high, with a crossbar from which hung a wooden ball about two inches in diameter. A wooden peg about four inches high stood under the ball, and the player had to swing the ball and try to knock down the peg. He offered me a free turn; I tried it and down went the peg, but when I wanted to try again, he forbade further practising. Instead, he offered me a turn for a penny, and promised me a gold watch, which he held to my ear to proved that it ticked. I paid my penny and tried, but missed. I was only eleven but I was sure that I had been swindled, although I could not see how it was done. In the evening I went back to watch at the same stall and saw a young farm labourer put up half a crown. The ball went round in a circle instead of swinging straight down. His mate also lost half a crown, and then I saw how it was worked. On the practice run, the structure stood free, but when the money was on, the man leant on one pole and inevitably, the ball was deflected. I could understand his doing it for half a crown, but not to take a penny from an eleven year old.

Other attractions were shooting galleries with ping pong balls dancing on water jets and the back of the gallery covered with bottles which could be broken by rapid fire. A goldfish could be won by throwing a ping pong ball into its bowl, but the fish usually died within a few days. There were also swings, chair-o-planes, roundabouts and the helter-skelter for rides.

Jacob Studt also showed the first cinema film to be seen in Poole, apologising in advance because the titles were in German. He hoped that we would enjoy the show, but it was predictably unintelligible. The entrance fee was three pence in the evenings and a penny on Saturdays. The first picture palace in the borough was opened in 1909 by Mr Holder in a small hall near the railway bridge in Salterns Road. Next year the 'pictures' came to Poole on a permanent basis with the opening of the Electric Theatre in the erstwhile Longfleet Congregational Church opposite Topp's corner. Later, films were shown at the Amity Hall accompanied by music hall turns. There were no cinemas open on Sundays until the late 1920's after a public ballot, when the Bournemouth Electric Theatre was the first to open on the Sabbath.

The Poole Electric Theatre was open on Saturday afternoons

Poole Electric Theatre.

particularly for children. On Fridays a cameraman could be seen on the outside balcony, turning the handle attached to a box pointed at the small crowd gathered in the street. We did not know that we were being filmed. The cinema specialised in serials which continued week after week for several months. At the end of each episode, Pearl White would be left tied to the railway line with the train approaching, or about to fall over a cliff, as the 'Continued next week' caption appeared. Saturday matinees cost 2^1/2d and the chief feature was always Cowboys and Indians. In spite of a notice saying 'No shouting. No stamping. No whistling.', the audience was far from restrained. They booed the villain and cheered the hero, shouted 'Look out! He's coming up behind you', yelled out the captions in unison, and if the pianist played a song they knew, sang at the top of their voices. They also stood on the seats and threw peanut shells on the floor. Quite often the ringleaders were thrown out into the street. I only managed to go a few times and then after a lot of pleading because it was normally out of bounds as unsuitable.

Although it was a great disappointment not to be able to see Pearl White being saved, I was allowed to go to entertainments organised by the Chapel where local talent performed. The great attraction was Mr George Stone, singer, actor and comedian. Once I remember a German band with a dancing bear on a chain playing outside the burial ground at Hunger Hill; it must have been about 1908. Then there was the organ grinder with a monkey in a red cap, and a barrel organ which played classical airs and music hall hits.

We had no live theatre in Poole and the best we could hope for was a touring company performing 'Murder in the Red Barn' or 'Sweeney Todd, the Demon Barber'. Sometimes there was a Punch and Judy show or an itinerant conjurer hired the Temperance Hall for an audience of children. The Amity Hall show consisted of performers singing popular songs like 'My Old Dutch' and 'Down at the old Bull and Bush', tap dancers, clog dancers, jugglers and magicians. It was third rate stuff, but the tickets cost only sixpence, nine pence and a shilling, and the show was considered better value than the Electric Cinema.

Outside, hoops and tops were our favourite pastimes, together with skipping, tipcat and marbles. There was also something called 'Parabola' which involved a piece of wood, three inches in diameter, with a 'V' cut into it. This was rolled on a string between two sticks, tossed into the air, and caught on the rebound. In season we played conkers, (which are named from the verb conquer), baking them in the oven to harden them. Some players, if they were telling the truth, had conkers that had been baked many times and had destroyed as many as a hundred lesser nuts. One boaster declared that he had a hundred and tenner, but I never managed more than a sixer. It was in fact a dangerous pastime, with the possibility of a nasty blow in the face, but the game was also the culmination of twelve months' watching and anticipation. Our main source of supply was the trees along Park Road from Middle Park Gates to Park Gates East. As winter gave way to spring, we watched the buds burst and form the long red candles that would give us our conkers. Gradually, the leaves turned to gold and fell to cover the footpath and be scuffed into the roadway, revealing the horseshoes and nails at the end of the stems. We watched carefully for the ripening nuts. There were two methods of collecting them, either to climb the tree, or to throw heavy pieces of wood into the branches to knock then down. Both of these drew down the wrath of Mr Palmer, the Head Park Keeper. Apparently we were supposed to wait below the tree until the nuts fell off of their own accord, which was really too much to ask. Fortunately, the only punishment was a severe reprimand and threats of fetching a policeman.

In the winter, Saturday afternoons were given over to football. At twelve, I played in a Poole schools soccer trial at Breakheart Lane, a football field off Fernside Road used by Longfleet St. Mary's. I usually played at inside left but there were already two very good boys in that position. One, Harold Cornibeer, was very good indeed and became one of Dorset's most capped players. I played at left back, a position totally hopeless for me because I could not kick the ball far enough when taking goal kicks. The game was a trial for the annual match, Poole boys versus Bournemouth boys, which was played at Eastlake in the pouring rain. Poole lost, one nil. Arthur Whittle played a 'blinder' in goal, Dennis Keene was at left back and Cornibeer had a very good game at inside left. Later Cornibeer joined Bournemouth Gasworks at eighteen and became one of the best forwards to represent the county. We had three senior teams, Poole, Longfleet St. Mary's and Bournemouth Gasworks, who played at Sterte, Breakheart Lane and Eastlake respectively. They all played in the Dorset League and Cup, and the English Amateur Cup, and admission was one shilling, (free after half time). At Eastlake, many a game was stopped by a tram conductor blowing his whistle from the top deck as he stopped the tram to see some of the match.

The phrase 'It's not all beer and skittles', came from the skittle alleys that could be found attached to most public houses. The alley was about twenty feet long with a wooden floor, and the game was

Chestnuts near Park Gates East, Poole Park.

played with ten skittles and three balls, the forerunner of modern ten pin bowling. It was a very rough affair, the sport of the working class which, combined with darts and generous consumption of the local brew, became the highlight of pub sporting activity.

One of the more stupid forms of entertainment before the first world war was a smoking concert. My father went to one and came home reeking of tobacco smoke. My mother was not amused because it took a very long time to remove the smell from his clothes. He also looked terrible, and as far as we could discover the participants simply smoked cigarettes, cigars and pipes solidly for about three hours while some kind of concert was in progress. He admitted that it had been almost impossible to see more than a few yards, and that there was a great deal of coughing. The good thing about the whole ridiculous business was that it put me off smoking for the rest of my life.

My father also belonged to an organisation called P.S.A., short for Pleasant Sunday Afternoon, held in the Skinner Street Congregational Church. The members sang hymns and subscribed a small sum each week, and at Christmas selected 'prizes' to the value of their contributions. I liked this because he bought books which suited me rather than himself, such as Dickens and Sir Walter Scott.

The Ancient Order of Rechabites owned the Temperance Hall in Hill Street and my mother, who was strictly teetotal, took me there on Wednesdays to meetings of the British Women's Temperance Association where we were warned about the evils of strong drink. We sang 'My drink is water bright / From the crystal spring', which was marvellous, but worried me because I knew of no crystal spring anywhere near Poole. However my family had already signed the pledge not to touch strong drink for the rest of our lives and we had a certificate hung up in the bedroom, and wore blue ribbons in our buttonholes to prove it.

Our home entertainment was an Edison phonograph which played His Master's Voice or Edison Bell cylindrical records rendering the voice of Caruso, Jenny Lind or Harry Lauder, and the bagatelle board, a primitive form of billiards. I made my first wireless set in 1922, knowing nothing whatever about the subject, except for some simple looking instructions in a copy of Amateur Radio. I started with a disc of cardboard about four inches in diameter with a hole in the middle on to which I wound the required number of lengths of insulated wire. At intervals, a wire was fed off to be connected to a semicircle of brass studs fastened to a Bakelite cover mounted on to a square wooden box. A Bakelite knob and a copper arm could be turned in a semicircle connected to a 'cat's whisker'. A length of wire with insulators stretched across the yard as an aerial, and a pair of headphones completed the set. At three o'clock in the afternoon the Savoy Orpheans and Havanna Bands broadcast from the Savoy Hotel in London, and when the set was ready I raced home from my job on my bicycle to find that it worked very successfully. The set lasted for several years and could be used by two people using one earphone each. In fact we heard the general election results of 1923, (when Freddy Guest lost his seat to Hall Caine) in this way. In the days before television, video, discos or pin-ball machines, the best kind of entertainment was the kind we made ourselves.

The 'Bournemouth Queen'.

A submarine for breaking up at Ballast Quay, 1920.

CHAPTER SEVEN

In 1918, I was indentured for five years to the Hamworthy Engineering Company as an engineering draughtsman, starting at 13s 9d a week, (3s 3d of which was war bonus). I became, I believe, a good draughtsman and was eventually put in charge of the progress department at £2 a week. One of my most interesting jobs was to take charge of the installation of a large semi-diesel engine into a steel four-masted schooner, the *Ballycorus*, moored at Hamworthy. Some of the proceedings were hilarious. Our first job was to put a steel bulkhead across the ship to make the engine room. The steel plates had been drilled, the angle iron uprights were in place, and on deck we had a hand blown forge. The blacksmith, who was acting as the riveter, was in the hold with his mate who was equipped with a bucket, a pair of tongs and a hand held dolly, (a heavy piece of steel three inches in diameter). Neither the smith nor his mate could see each other. Standing on the deck, I heated the rivet until it was white hot, grabbed it with a pair of tongs, and shouting 'Coming down', dropped it down a ventilator into the hold where in theory the mate caught it in his bucket and pushed it through the hole in the plate and the angle, shank first. He then put the dolly against the head of the rivet, and shouted 'Right' whereupon the blacksmith, Tommy Tucker, hit the rivet into place. Generally it worked very well, but if the rivet failed to enter the bucket and ended up in the bilge water, or if it was not hot enough, we had to start again. More dangerously, if Tommy hit the rivet before the dolly was in place, the red hot missile went hurtling across the hold into the stern of the ship. The mate and I alternated in operating the forge and the bucket, but I much preferred the job on deck because it was safer.

Eventually the ship was ready. The captain, Henry Pulsford, came from a Poole seafaring family, and his sons later became captains or crew of coastal vessels. He brought the *Ballycorus* off the hard at the Haven at high tide, swung her head to starboard, and started the engine. The captain ordered 'Three blasts on the siren'. I pulled the cord and was gratified to find that it worked. I had been promised that I could sail on her voyage to Antwerp as super cargo, but my boss persuaded me not to go. Later, Henry Pulsford changed the ship's name to *Henford*, which was a pity; *Ballycorus* was much more romantic.

The end of the war had brought some poverty to Poole as men and women were discharged from the forces and from wartime industry and found it difficult to find work. In 1921, unemployment pay was introduced at a weekly rate of fourteen shillings, and the price of the insurance stamp was raised by a few pence. New work schemes came into being and the James Smith Company rented Ballast Quay to break up submarines and destroyers. Many men had to be trained in the use of oxyacetylene torches. Everything useful was preserved and I bought a lot of material for the Hamworthy Engineering Company.

By the 1920's, violence and war seemed to be behind us. In 1920, I crossed the Channel on board the *Bournemouth Queen* on a day excursion to Cherbourg. She left Bournemouth pier at 9.00am. and a westerly wind caused her to list to port for the whole sixty miles. Some people were seasick within a few minutes. The crew worked hard with buckets and mops, but it became an uncomfortable trip for those recumbent in the saloon, knowing that there was no other way to get back to Bournemouth. The ship was a coal-burning paddle steamer and ash from her funnel dropped on to the deck which was quite open. At Cherbourg we wandered about the town for about an hour and I tried out my schoolboy French on the shopkeepers, buying a napkin ring decorated with the coat of arms of the port, while a friend of mine was given a visiting card by an attractive young lady. As

Beating the Bounds celebrations, 1922.

the ship's siren sounded, we all made our way back on board, except for one man who was nearly too late and had to jump for the stern rail as the ship moved away. On the return journey, we listed to starboard and even more passengers took to the saloon. I have always been a good sailor, and the idea of landing in France was worth the journey, but it could hardly be described as a pleasure trip.

Dorothy, my future wife, and I met in 1921 on the open air badminton court of the Central Hotel, Market Street. We were eighteen and with the world to be explored we were drawn inevitably into a lifelong partnership that never faltered. At eighty two we could look back on a lifetime that held no sorrows we could not overcome, and adventures that seemed impossible to contemplate in those blissful and romantic years.

We both came from fanatically religious families and our lives, quite independently, followed the same pattern. Grandfather Bristowe was a devout Baptist who travelled with his pony and gig to preach in nearby Dorset villages. My father and mother followed this religious bent, and in the normal course of events I would have been baptised at sixteen or seventeen. However, when I was twelve, they changed chapels and became Congregationalists who baptise their followers as babies. I was therefore never baptised at all. Dorothy's family was Wesleyan and had been so from the days of the famous Charles, but they too changed and became Quakers, the one out of all the multitudinous sects that make up the Christian religion that I would choose for its simplicity and sincerity. Our lives from the age of four to nineteen consisted of meetings or chapel on Sundays from nine in the morning to nine thirty at night with weekday services as well. Our subsequent backsliding from this Victorian style of Christianity was inevitable, but perhaps we at least absorbed knowledge of the difference between right and wrong.

When I was eighteen, our church was in trouble because they needed a Sunday School secretary and were finding it very difficult to persuade anyone to take on the position. The Sunday School Superintendent was a dear old gentleman who sported a beard, and as a small child, I imagined him to be the image of God. He decided that I would make an ideal secretary and approached my mother about it. She was most anxious that I should accept and made an appointment for me to be at the Superintendent's house at 6 pm. the next day. I protested without any success and the following day found me reluctantly walking to the house in Longfleet Road. I tapped nervously, and not too heavily, on the door and no-one came, so I went home and said that there had been no answer. My mother was sceptical, and the next evening the old gentleman came to our house; he cried on my shoulder, and I was lost. I did the job for eighteen months, marking attendance cards with a blue star, keeping records, and attending Sunday School at ten in the morning and two in the afternoon. Dorothy helped me with the paperwork.

My major effort was to organise a Sunday School outing to the New Forest in the summer of 1921, the brain child of Mr Edward Short. At eighteen, I was not too happy about the whole thing, imagining lost children, accidents and sickness, but all went well. We must have had over two hundred pupils with teachers and church officials, and for transport we hired Royal Blue Coaches of Bournemouth. The coaches, all open, arrived outside the Gas Company's offices at nine o'clock, and we went off in convoy to a forest clearing near Lyndhurst. The catering committee excelled themselves and the sports committee organised races and games. It seemed that a good time was had by all, until the time came to board the buses for home. The coaches were to be there at four o'clock, but only two arrived at the appointed time and we sent off the youngest children. A phone call to Royal Blue assured us that the rest were on their way, and sure enough, one more arrived. It was then quite obvious that they had been sent on other engagements, and as one arrived back at the garage, it was hurriedly sent out to us. I stayed to the end when the last coach arrived, well after nine o'clock. We reached Poole just before midnight to find anxious parents looking out for their children; I could only assure them that nobody had been left in the New Forest. It must have been the most ambitious Sunday School outing in the history of the church, as they usually just walked to Sterte or Poole Park. I resigned before another such adventure could be arranged.

On Sundays, at eighteen, I used to wear a bowler hat and blue pin-striped suit and carry a silver knobbed cane. In summer, a straw hat was substituted for the bowler. Looking back it seems incredible, but I was one of four who dressed like this and joined the parading round the town. The girls also dressed elegantly on Sundays and always bought a new hat at Easter, traditionally an Easter bonnet. With the advent of the motor car, bowlers, boaters and large hats disappeared and travel replaced promenading. The 'Flapper' appeared, skirts were shortened and women's hair was bobbed or shingled. At eighteen, Dorothy's hair reached her waist and all suggestions that she should have it bobbed were sternly refused by her father. At twenty one, exerting her rights as an adult, she had the large bun of hair cut off. It was kept for a few years and eventually sold to a wig-maker. Her father was not pleased.

That year we took our first holiday together in Brighton, Dorothy to stay with her aunt and uncle, and I to sleep in a nearby house. We went by train, changing at Southampton. The holiday was a great success. We patronised both piers, paying a penny to see 'What the butler saw', and listened to the military band playing the music hall hit of the year which was 'Yes, we have no bananas'. We sat in deck chairs to see the Pierrot show and dropped pennies into the collecting box for the Punch and Judy. The beach was hard and pebbly, unlike the golden sands of Shell Bay and Studland, with cockle and whelk stalls sheltering under the high promenade. We walked along the downs eastward and went to Hove to see the Australian eleven play Sussex at cricket. This was a side of ex-soldiers including Gregory and Macdonald, the demon fast bowlers, who were such a success on tour. Looking back, I think they were the first of the bodyline bowlers, although Larwood and Voce eventually got the blame. Like all holiday makers, we walked through Brighton Pavilion, the dream child of the Prince Regent, dating from 1794 when sea bathing became popular. Bathing boxes drawn by horses were still there, and we used them - separately. In 1922, we became engaged.

There was some disagreement at this time as to whether Lord Wimborne owned the land along the shores of Poole Bay to high or low water mark. A footpath from the harbour shore to Arne had been used by Poole men from time immemorial, and when it was fenced off by the Lord of the Manor, a party of local enthusiasts put their rights to the test by a planned expedition. This led to the Beating of the Bounds ceremony organised by H. P. Smith and the Society of Poole Men. They set off every year from Poole Quay and landed at strategic points around the harbour, proclaiming the boundaries as given in the charter of Poole and accompanied by a gang of pirates flying the skull and crossbones, flags which Dorothy and I were involved in making and painting.

Every year, the D'Oyly Carte Opera Company held a season at the old Theatre Royal in Bournemouth, and we became Gilbert and Sullivan fans. We rode in the tram to Bournemouth Square for five pence and sat in the gallery for a shilling each. Unfortunately, the last tram left the Square for Poole exactly at the time that the performance finished and this meant that we had to leave early and miss the final chorus, or catch a later tram that went only to the Ashley Road depot, four miles from Poole. Usually we caught the late tram and walked home via Constitution Hill overlooking the harbour. With a full moon over the English Channel, we could see the winking lights of the town below us and beyond, Brownsea Island and the mouth of the harbour. Sometimes a collier would be steaming down the main channel, her red port light showing clearly, following the path of the mine sweepers of 1916 as far as Bar Buoy whose light we could see on the horizon. The lights in line gave its direction, and away to the east, the bright lights of Bournemouth turned the sky to

A performance by Parkstone Operatic Society.

crimson. This view from Constitution Hill led Edward, Prince of Wales, to exclaim in 1890 'Ah, Mentone', and from this remark, Mentone Road in Parkstone was named. From here we still had around three miles to walk, arriving home about 11.30 pm.

We also joined the Parkstone Operatic Society and sang in 'Cigarette', 'Les Cloches de Cornville', 'Dorothy' and 'Miss Hook of Holland' first in the St. Peter's school in Parkstone, and then in the Theatre Royal in Bournemouth. The Society entered the Bournemouth Festival of Music but the men's performance of 'Down among the Dead Men' was unplaced. The judge said that we were a plucky little choir because we sang without music, but he thought that we did not really appreciate the finer points of the piece, and did not seem to be acquainted with 'the dead men' which were the empty bottles under the table after a drinking party. The girls won their section with 'Annie Laurie', a song which we can always sing when driving along.

Dorothy's father was one of the original Quakers who helped to form the Poole Adult School which we joined in 1922. The school had its inaugural meeting in 1906 in the Friends' Meeting House in Lagland Street, its aims being to teach working class men to read and write, to hold a short religious service consisting chiefly of singing hymns, and to recruit knowledgeable citizens to talk for half an hour on any interesting subject. The meetings were held at nine o'clock on Sunday mornings. Originally, the Meeting House was crowded and illiterate men did learn to read and write, alcoholics were reformed and hungry men were fed, but by the time we joined, the meetings were usually attended by about twenty people. The audience was still chiefly from the working class, and the meetings still followed the traditional pattern of religious service and half hour talks. We had electricians and plumbers, an expert on the safety razor, a monetary reformist who proposed a kind of social credit, and even a man who told us how to bath a canary. The frivolous were offset by historians, philosophers, a phrenologist, town councillors, reformists, and anyone who cared to stand up and talk. I learned a great deal and it gave me my first attempt at public speaking. By the time that we ceased to attend in 1928, I could make impromptu speeches and propose votes of thanks, which later led to my giving lectures on my hobbies, travels, and any prepared subject to interested groups.

When Dorothy left her Quaker boarding school, she was advised by the Headmistress not to attend football/sports matches, but she accepted my enthusiasm for the game, and accompanied me to many matches. We supported Boscombe for several years, paying a shilling entrance fee to stand on a bank of gravel with a corrugated iron fence behind us. In the 1950's and '60's, we saw several cup finals at

Poole Adult School. Second from left in the front row is E. E. Kendal, the author's father-in-law.

Wembley and attended international matches including England versus the Rest of the World.

We also followed cricket, watching Hampshire play at Dean Park. During the August Festival, many organisations would erect marquees where their members could have lunch and bring their ladies to afternoon tea. These included the Bournemouth Corporation, the Gentlemen's Club, the Sport's Club, the Y.M.C.A. and the Chamber of Commerce. Their guests sat in deck chairs and waiters served them with tea and coffee, while we, the general public, sat on wooden planks. Two beer tents were erected, and from trestle tables, half pints of beer were served to be consumed inside or just outside the tent. No beer was taken to the seats. The ground was patrolled by two policemen, and if a spectator removed his shirt, he was immediately told to put it on again. The amateur players came from the pavilion and the professionals from a wooden hut, and sat on a wooden staging when not playing. We saw the great Philip Mead, George Brown, who kept wicket, bowled and batted for England, and the Hon Lionel Tennyson, who captained the side. Later we saw Larwood and Voce at Nottingham, and Bradman's Australian side, playing England at Leeds and Manchester, where Hobbs and Sutcliff opened for England.

Before the first world war, badminton was a game played by the leisured classes, particularly sahibs and their ladies in India. When war was declared, the Dorset Regiment was sent to India where the troops learned the game, and brought it back to England. Every hall that was large enough was used, the first one in Poole being at the Skinner Street Congregational Church. Tom Kingsbury, who had been in India, organised the club, and at seventeen, I found that I had a reasonable affinity for the game. Instead of switching to tennis in the summer, I played badminton on an outdoor court behind the Central Hotel in Market Street. Dorothy also joined the club and we 'went out together' and played badminton for the next eighteen years. The game grew rapidly and was played at the Antelope Hall, the Poole Gymnasium, the Oddfellows' Hall and in most of the schools. Dorothy and I graduated to the Parkstone Olympic Club and the Bournemouth Club, and for several years played in the English Counties Championships for Dorset. In 1938, I also played in the All-England competition. We both played hockey in a mixed team for Poole Nomads, and found that a game of squash rackets could be fitted into our life-style more easily than badminton. A half hour game was sufficient, with a swim in the hotel pool, although we had to travel to Bournemouth to find a court.

These happy courtship years were hard times for some. The general strike of 1926 affected Poole considerably. Southern

Roadways, a haulage firm in West Quay Road, took charge of all road transport, and any independent hauliers who would work were told to report. The strike lasted only ten days, but the coal miners continued for another six months, and parties of six miners could often be seen walking slowly along the High Street, singing to raise money. They looked destitute and hungry but they could sing well, and *Cwm Rhondda* helped to fill their collecting boxes. The miners eventually gave in and went back to work on the owners' terms.

Two years later, on the 14th July 1928, Dorothy and I were married in the Quaker Meeting House in Poole. It was the first marriage there for eighty years and the last, because the lovely old seventeenth century building then became a youth club run by the Local Education Authority. Unfortunately, its members simply wrecked the interior, which I thought was sacrilege. One evening I happened to be passing and went in to see why there was so much noise, to find the boys playing football, kicking the ball against the walls and ceiling. The plain wooden seats had disappeared. Between 1921 and 1928 we had set out to save £500 which we managed with a little

My wedding, 1928.

to spare, and were able to build a two storey house in Fernside Road for £830 including the land. Electricity had not yet reached the outskirts of the town, but we had the house wired and used oil lamps for two years rather than have gas pipes installed for lighting.

We used a Morris Cowley belonging to my father-in-law for our honeymoon. It had a canvas hood, mica side screens, artillery wheels and a bulb horn, and boiled all the way up the hills of Chideock and Charmouth, just managing to climb Porlock and Countisbury Hills in North Devon. It was the first time I had driven a car any great distance and the idea was to cover as many miles as possible, looking at a place and then moving on. We managed it in two weeks which meant travelling each day and staying only one night in each place.

Interior of Friends' Meeting House, Poole.

CHAPTER EIGHT

L eaving engineering in 1923, I had entered the haulage business with my father, while Dorothy had an executive position with Poole Pottery which she had held since 1921, when she became their first staff member. The pottery was first established in the late 19th century making floor tiles and architectural ceramics. By the early 20th century, tableware was being manufactured as a sideline and in 1921, Cyril Carter, a descendent of the firm's founder, decided to set up a subsidiary company to make pottery in partnership with Harold Stabler and John Adams. The company, known as Carter, Stabler and Adams, (or C.S.A.), occupied the buildings at East Quay which had been part of the Carter faience department. The factory consisted of a lane running from East Quay Road to the Quay, with a series of small rooms, some connected to each other with wooden staircases, running up the outside to the second floor. On the other side of the lane were two huge muffle kilns and various rooms for sorting biscuit, (the fired but unglazed pottery). Some of the brickwork of the buildings came from demolished kilns and still showed clinker from the ovens. Tradition had it that Owen Carter, son of the firm's founder, did some of the brick laying in his spare time.

John Adams and Dorothy Kendall arrived on the first day in the summer of 1921. He was the Managing Director, and she was the typist, the only staff member, with an initial salary of 15s per week. There were also a few workers including a thrower, a wedger, a caster, slip and glaze workers, and a few paintresses. Within four weeks, Dorothy had been made Production Manager at a salary of £4 per week. Her job was to supervise the production of pots according to the orders that were received, and this consisted of detailing the orders, ensuring that the right kind of biscuit was always on the warehouse shelves, trying to get the whole of an order glazed and fired at the same time, and the most difficult of all, holding a half completed order until the pieces that had failed were replaced. The main problem was that an order from a London store could consist of possibly two hundred pieces, all different, and each one had to be made specially, and carefully listed. When a kiln full of hundreds of pieces met with a problem, it was extremely difficult to get an order away complete. Smaller items, however, like jampots, egg cups, cruets and small vases, were a stock production and the selection was left to the warehouse staff. When an order came in for, say, £10 worth of small pottery, things went very smoothly.

In 1924, John Adams was asked to design and make the war memorial for the city of Durban, and Harold and Phoebe Stabler came to Poole to do the modelling. A scaffolding was erected about nine feet high, and they proceeded to model the figures which included two angels. William Bryant and his staff in Carter's faience department made the moulds and fired the blocks, and the various glazes were prepared by Ernest Legg for C.S.A. The gloss firing took place in one of the Carter muffle kilns. To everyone's consternation, the faces of the angels came out blue. Ernest Legg admitted the possibility that he had made a mistake but also suggested that the glazers may have been to blame. The Stablers had to chisel off the glaze from the faces, a long and laborious task, and then smooth away the chisel marks from the hard biscuit. The faces were reglazed and the blocks successfully refired.

Dorothy's problem was that there was never enough time during the day to complete the preparation necessary for production. As a friend of the Production Manager, I found myself at her home in the evenings, sorting out orders and making lists for throwing, slipping, glazing and firing. Of course, I was not being paid, but strangely enough I rather enjoyed it, and we did this several times a week at least for the first year. In the meantime I came to know the Carters, the Stablers and the Adams at works dances, outings and occasional private dinners. When we were married in 1928, Mrs Adams suggested that I be offered Dorothy's job. This was the respectable job that my mother had wanted for me, and I accepted, staying for fifteen years until the war decided that I must change. Starting work on 30th July 1928, my experience with the homework meant that I was already very familiar with the problems of production. Dorothy stayed on for three years managing the painting shops until Barbara, our daughter, was born in 1932, returning to work between 1937 and 1939.

Until 1930, Carters' representatives were our only contact with our customers, but I then travelled England for twelve months to gain experience of customers' requirements, returning as Works Manager. Our first full-time representative was Neild Adams who came to us from Pyrex and rapidly increased the demand for Poole pottery. The company came through the depression of the 1930's reasonably well, and by 1932 we were working at full capacity with twenty six paintresses and thirty clay workers and staff. The young paintresses, many straight from school, were first engaged in making pounces

Paintresses at work.

Gertie Gilham, 1936.

which involved tracing the design on to transparent paper. The outline was then pricked with a needle and the paper was placed on the glazed pot and dusted with a bag of charcoal, leaving a dotted outline. The paintress decided the number of units required, although there was a degree of improvisation because of the varied shapes and the free-hand nature of the work. After a few months, the trainees commenced painting the small posies of flowers on jampots and all the smaller items.

The youngsters also conducted the visitors around the works and there is no doubt that they did very well with tips. One visitor came back the next day to say that he had inadvertently given one girl two gold sovereigns and I had the delicate job of recovering them. It is interesting to remember that only two men were painting during the first twenty five years. E. E. Strickland, an artist with Carter's, and a young man named Way who was a house painter, were both very good. Neither stayed for any length of time, and the girls probably adapted better to the constant repetition.

Mrs Adams had been designing from the beginning and she introduced a new body, giving us a cream surface and eliminating the necessity for a cream slip to be applied to the red ball clay body. She also introduced the spot edge which became the feature of all the decorated ware. From about 1925, Gertie Gilham became chief thrower, succeeding her sister, who had been at the pottery with Owen Carter. One of the main attractions for the visitors was the large throwing wheel which was turned by a girl operating a hand wheel about five feet in diameter. This was connected to the throwing wheel by a rope, and there had to be good co-operation between the wheel turner and the thrower to get the right revolutions. People came back year after year to the pottery to say 'Are you still turning that thing?'. The small items were thrown on electrically operated wheels.

Nield Adams' ability as a representative was showing excellent results, and my twelve months travelling experience meant that we at the pottery were aware of some of the difficulties associated with the retail trade. I found customers with stock which they had held since the days of Owen Carter, ten years before, which was quite unsaleable. In one case I smashed the whole of the stock and replaced it with the current production. On one occasion, the manager of a large city store was very upset because he was being undersold by another retailer, although he was displaying Poole pottery at sale prices. I was surprised to find that his sale prices were very much higher than those we felt to be reasonable. I had the greatest difficulty in getting both parties to come to an agreement. There was also the problem as to whether one retailer should have the sole rights of selling Poole pottery in his own particular area.

Towards the end of the depression, a firm making ovenware went out of business and their team of representatives, which travelled the whole of Great Britain, were recommended to us. Nield Adams was now well established in his job, but it was suggested that the new group could visit every customer at intervals of a few months and sell our product in small lots of £5 or £10 at our selection, and that this would simplify the processing of orders. I was not at all happy with the proposition. It would make Nield Adams' position very difficult and would not be at all to the liking of the large stores. In the end it was agreed that Nield Adams would continue to sell in the normal way, but that the new people would endeavour to place the pottery all over Great Britain with small retailers and arts and craft shops. Initially we were overwhelmed with £5 orders, and our stock was completely depleted, but the repeat orders did not arrive and the scheme was abandoned.

We had opened a showroom and restaurant and invited visitors to tour the works. This made us a viable part of the Carter group because in the holiday period we had hundreds of people crowding into the rather inadequate rooms and walking up and down the outside staircases. They were then taken to the showroom where they bought up all the second quality pieces. This meant that we were receiving wholesale prices for pottery which would otherwise would have been sent out to customers at greatly reduced rates for the January sales. It helped to maintain quality by providing a market for the 'rejects'.

John Adams insisted that the glaze, which we knew as pot facing, was applied thickly, giving the ware its high quality appearance. The biscuit needed to be fired to a certain porosity, but if there were hot spots in the large muffle kilns and it was overfired, we were plagued with a crawling of the glaze which could throw our order sequence into chaos. J. A. was also a great experimenter. We once loaded the small muffle kiln in Dorey's yard with Chinese stoneware, hoping to reach a temperature of 1350 degrees. We fired it with oak logs, and as fast as I threw in a log, it burst into flames and disintegrated immediately. When we took down the front wall of the kiln, we found that we had melted the bats, the props and the pots, and even the side wall of the kiln. This was a tragedy because J. A. had been experimenting with the ash of rhododendron logs in the glaze and the result had been magnificent. Alas, we saved only a few small pieces.

By the mid 1930's, we were an important part of the group, and were contributing to the profits, but it was obvious that the premises were inadequate. We needed to install a tunnel kiln instead of the muffles, and a new site at Hamworthy was being considered. It was decided to make tea and dinnerware, the first comprising the normal pieces, the latter consisting of two covered vegetable dishes, a sauce boat, two small covered bowls, six dinner, pudding and side plates, plus three oval dishes, the largest of which would take the Christmas turkey. We lacked the facilities to jolley the plates and dishes, and so we bought the biscuit from Johnsons of Stoke on Trent. We were able to make the biscuit for the teasets and were now involved in the traditional mass production of pottery.

As well as making dinner and teaware, we continued to make the traditional decorated pottery, but we found that matchings were a great problem. People valued their Poole pottery so much that if a jam pot lid was broken, they wanted it replaced, in some cases many years after the original purchase. They took the pieces to a retailer who posted them to us with an order. As the pottery was hand made, we had to be extremely careful that the new lid would fit the original jam pot, and it had to go through every process as a special piece. It was my job to analyse the contents of each kiln, and keep records showing the loss in percentages. I can remember the call of the sorters, 'One cracked, one crawled, one chipped', and the ring of a wooden ruler shaken in the mouth of a vase, or the dull thud of a cracked pot.

Dorothy and I organised the London exhibitions. These were held in Gieve's Gallery, Bond Street, in September, at the British Industries Fair at Olympia in February, and at the Chelsea flower show in May. They gave us a chance to spend some weeks away from the never ending routine, and to enjoy the sophistication of London. At the British Industries Fair we regularly met members of the Royal Family who visited the stand, and on one occasion I discussed the various pieces with Queen Mary. The Duke of Kent and the Prince of Wales visited us every year, and J. A. once entertained Queen Mary and King George VI and their retinue. One day at Gieve's Gallery, during a dull period, I remember arranging eight vases in a row and playing 'God save the King' with a ruler.

Exhibition at Gieve's Gallery, London.

The year 1935 was probably our best, but trouble lay ahead. J. A. developed pleurisy and was away for nearly three months. I now had the responsibility of the whole works including the office management, production, and the dispatch of orders. J. A. had introduced an experimental new design of vases which consisted of white pots with modern shaped lugs, glazed in blue or green. The glazers had no experience of the process and without his supervision it was a near disaster, with blue and green fingerprints on the white glaze. We abandoned the production until J. A. recovered. When he returned, we continued to prosper. The depression was well behind us and visitors continued to arrive in their hundreds.

In early 1936, J. A. and Mrs Adams separated and she eventually married Cyril Carter. In the interests of the company, all three continued their association with the business, although Mrs Adams was away from the studio for about eight months. One Saturday morning at the British Industries Fair that year, J. A. asked Dorothy and me to stay for the afternoon because Mrs Adams and Mr Carter wished to see the exhibition, and he could not stay because of the nine months decree nisi. We stayed on, and that evening dined at the Kensington Palace Hotel and had a box at the Lyric Theatre, Hammersmith, to see John Gay's 'The Beggar's Opera'. It was a night to remember. At Gieve's Gallery, an attractive lady was introduced to J. A., and three months later, he invited Dorothy and me to dinner and told us that he was about to be married again.

Some key workers were with C.S.A. for many years. Frank Wright, originally from Stoke on Trent, came to Poole in the early 1920's, and was in charge of the casting production. He was a skilled mouldmaker. In the first World War, he had been a sergeant in the Staffordshire Regiment, and had been taken prisoner in the retreat from Mons. He left the pottery at the outbreak of the second World War having to have a leg amputated through leg ulcers caused by his war service. Fred Stout, a local lad, was assistant mould maker, and Sam Wilson, also from Stoke on Trent, controlled the casting, together with Lily Brown, a local girl. Syd Edwards was fireman. He had served as a stoker in coal-fired warships in the first World War. His job was to handle the huge muffle kilns, judging the temperature through a spy hole, watching and melting cones, and shovelling coal at regular intervals throughout the night. He left us on the outbreak of the war to join the Pioneer Corps. Ernest Hustler, a veteran of the Dorset Regiment that sailed up the Tigris to the relief of Kut, was our kiln setter. He too was with us for about 20 years and his assistant was Richard Damon.

Ruth Paveley was with the pottery from the early 1920's, and stayed for nearly 20 years. She became head paintress, and was

Ruth Pavely, 1936.

awarded the O.B.E. under the Industrial Awards Scheme. Phyllis Way came to the pottery straight from school. She became a maker of pounces, conducted visitors around the works, and became an excellent paintress. She then became the competent manageress of the showroom, handling the hundreds of visitors who at times swarmed all over the works demanding service. She also helped with the B.I.F. exhibition at Olympia for several years. Leslie Elsdon became chief glaze sprayer when Ernest Baggaley changed the system. He became very skilled and did a great deal to improve the quality of the ware. Margaret Holder was a very talented young woman who designed the ship plates for which Arthur Bradbury of Sandbanks supplied the original drawings. She handled all the new designs, adapting them to the various shapes, and her painting technique was superb. We were all rather shocked when she resigned to take up an office career.

Jimmy Soper was our turner, a dextrous lad who could whip the base from a clay pot, shaping the ridge with a piece of flat steel. He left us to go to Branksome, but he returned after a few years. Jack Eyers was the packer in 1921 and he was followed by Harry Bishton who came to us from Carter's where he was a box maker. After a few years he returned to Carter's and I engaged Arthur Dorey who came from Kingston, in the hills above Corfe Castle. I first met him when I played cricket for Carter's in the Wareham and District League and we needed a good batsman. He was a tall young man with huge hands and he helped us to victory in the Wyatt Cup when he made 75 against Wareham in Poole Park. He became a very good packer.

In the early days, several typists came to work for us but none of them stayed very long because they were unable to stand the rigours of a busy office. In the mid 1920's, Beatrice Bibby came and controlled a very efficient office. Steve Power was a character. He was employed by Carter's as a boiler man and his boiler was situated at the entrance to the works in East Quay Road. When he was not feeding the boiler, he stood in his doorway, greeting everyone who entered, as a self appointed welcomer. My first words every day were 'Morning Steve', and most people greeted him, including the directors who responded to his 'Morning Sir' and usually stopped to talk for a few moments. Always cheerful and liked by the girls, he gave the impression of having worked there for at least 50 years and was always ready to set visitors in the right direction in spite of the fact that the entrance was well sign-posted. He was still working there when I left in 1942, but probably left after modernisation since his boiler would have been obsolete.

Carter's Flower Show had been an annual event from time immemorial. It was held in the grounds of Carter's Almshouses at Hamworthy and engendered a great rivalry in competitions for flowers, vegetables and handicrafts. As with all such shows, grave doubts were sometimes expressed as to whether certain vegetables could possibly have come from a competitor's allotment. I once won first prize for runner beans. The works sports were fiercely contested. They included a walking race, three times round the field, which was always won by Harry Matthews from Whiteworks. We once ran a dog race, open to any kind of dog, contested over one length of the field. Each dog was held by a handler with the owner shouting encouragement from the finishing line. The race was won by Mrs. Carter's Airedale. We were a contented group in the days when those with a steady job held on to it, and very few people left until the war was declared in 1939.

CHAPTER NINE

In the early years of our married life, the bicycle gave us our freedom; Dorothy's a modern machine with dressguard, bell and brakes, and mine a second hand job costing ten shillings. Both had acetylene lamps. We cycled to Sandbanks at the mouth of the harbour, crossing the ferry to Shell Bay from the Haven Hotel, where stood the wooden mast from which Marconi sent his first wireless messages to the Isle of Wight, and sped along the hard sand at low tide to Studland and Corfe Castle. We explored the harbour shores from Lilliput to Stoke's Lake where the curlews thrust their long curved beaks into the soft grey sand, and the gulls watched patiently at the water's edge, standing on one leg and preening their feathers. We cycled to Arne and Shipstall from Wareham at the mouth of the River Frome, and followed the River Puddle on foot to its junction with the Frome, fancying that we had found the place where Canute landed his longships. We sailed in Trumpy Gough's fishing boat to Studland and sometimes had to walk back to Shell Bay because of the easterly wind which blew angrily, sending breakers on to the shore.

We went to Sandbanks by Harvey's or Gondolier motor boats, (some of which went to Dunkirk in 1940), and swam on the 'rough

The 'Monarch' off the Quay.

side', that is the Channel side, of the peninsula. Sometimes, in the height of comparative luxury, we went to Bournemouth or Swanage and even round the Isle of Wight on the paddle steamer 'Bournemouth Queen', which in 1945, as a patrol boat on the River Thames under the command of a Poole man, Tom Sherrin, shot down a German Heinkel. We also made the day long trip to Torquay on the twin funnelled 'Monarch', returning in dense fog to pick up the Shambles lightship, the blast of whose foghorn brought handclaps and cheers from the passengers for the captain's navigation.

As our prosperity increased, we bought our first car, a Singer Sports. It was said to be 8.9 horsepower and cost £125, but it was not really a sports car at all since the makers had simply put a two-seater body on to the standard chassis and moulded the rear end to a point. It was painted in a tasteful grey and green and was marvellous in fine weather. In woolly hats and scarves we managed a maximum speed of 40 m.p.h., but wet weather brought its problems because the hood was useless and we spent a great deal of time mopping out water. Nevertheless, it sufficed. Its tiny boot would hold a tent and poles with the odd frying pan and saucepan, ground sheets and a few sacks and bedding. On one trip, we camped at Durdle Door, where it rained for a week. We fished in the rain, swam in the rain, and picked a bucketful of mushrooms. Finally, in a heavy downpour, we threw the tent, bedding, kitchen utensils and the remaining food into the boot, and drove home in bare feet. But when did the rain stop anybody? At every opportunity we would set off, camping at West Bay, near

Bridport and round the shores of the harbour. We bought a better tent and spent weekends and holidays fishing off West Bay for pout whiting, spinning for mackerel and pollack, and catching prawns in a Bridport ring net. A fortnight on Berry Head in Devon brought continuous rain but it did not deter us.

Driving in those days was a very different experience from today. The first time that I saw traffic lights was in 1923 when I was driving a one ton truck in Bristol. They were quite a surprise. I had a vague idea about their function and knew enough to stop on the red signal and move on the green. I do not remember any lights in the town of Poole, and it was many years before they appeared, the first probably being at the *Shah of Persia* crossroads. The first mobile policeman in the town was a motor-cyclist who followed commercial vehicles, checking speeds, and he had the reputation of being very fair, allowing the driver to know that he was following. After a few years, police cars arrived, but they too were easily identified. My only misdemeanours in sixty two years of driving consisted of being fined five shillings for covering the number plate of a truck by driving with the tailboard down, and five shillings for not having a driving mirror on my first small car. In court the policeman said, looking at his notebook, 'When questioned, the defendant said 'I had one but it fell off'.

Dorothy and I had always been interested in sea angling and we found that whiting shoaled off Bournemouth pier after dark. One evening about seven o'clock, we tried our luck with three friends. The pier attendant had locked the gates, but we climbed over and fished from the lower deck until about ten o'clock. We were very successful and we tried it for several weeks. One night, however, we were caught. It was a bright, moonlit night. We saw the man lock the gates and waited until he went away and then started to climb over, ladies first. Two were over and we three men were about to follow when the man came back. He told us that no women were allowed on the pier after dark, and was unmoved by our argument that the women were wearing slacks. 'I don't care what they're wearing. No women on the pier after dark'. So we waited and when we were certain that he had gone home, we went back and climbed the gates again, deciding that it was unlikely that he would come out to the lower deck to investigate in the dark. We managed to fish there for the rest of the summer of 1930.

All this changed when Barbara was born on 30th May, 1932. On the afternoon of the 29th, it was raining. The nurse was installed in the spare bedroom and everything was ready, but Dorothy was restless. Nurse Tilley, in a blue starched uniform and white headdress, was efficient, firm and no small woman. Taking complete charge, she ordered us off. 'Out you go, both of you'. 'Where?', I asked meekly.

The beach at Shore Road, Sandbanks.

'Out in the car. Anywhere'. and so we went. We drove to Wareham and on towards the famous Puddle villages, Puddletown, Tolpuddle and Piddlehinton. The villagers could never make up their minds whether they were Puddles or Piddles and held a meeting to decide it once and for all. After lengthy discussion it was decided to leave the matter as it had always been, and so we still have Piddletrenthide, Affpuddle, Bryantspuddle and Turnerspuddle, or Piddle as the whim takes the inhabitants or the cartographers. On this occasion we were looking for rushes and water plants for a garden pool, and found a suitable creek, (or was it a puddle?). Certainly we found some small water lily plants and rushes, and paddled around in the mud, putting the plants in a wet sack. Then the rain really came down. Dorothy insisted on driving home as I had lost a shoe in the mud. Her extended figure pressed hard against the steering wheel, but she really could drive a car. As we entered the front door the pains started, and Barbara was born about six hours later. We always said that the birth certificate could easily have recorded the place of birth as the River Piddle, but it did not. She was born in the double bed in the front upstairs room of our house in Fernside Road.

Her arrival slowed down our activities, as a tent in the rain was no place for a baby. Instead, we rented a chalet on the seaward side of Sandbanks from the Poole Corporation. It was on the sea front and the bathing was excellent. Barbara crawled into the water at twelve months, could dog paddle at two and could swim a few strokes at three. We kept the chalet for several years, spending as much of the summer as possible lazing on the beach and swimming at every opportunity. The Singer could just manage to carry the three of us, Barbara on Dorothy's lap or standing close to the wind screen. After a year or two, we moved further afield to visit the places we had seen in the previous decade. We paddled and swam, picked primroses, bluebells and yellow stonecrop from the dry stone walls of Purbeck and in the winter, gathered hips and haws and holly for Christmas.

My first attempts at photography came about because Dorothy owned a quarter plate camera, named an Instantograph, dated 1899. It had a black cloth and brass lens which was covered by a leather cap, and used quarter glass plates. After focusing, exposure consisted of removing the cap and counting five. The plate was developed in a dish with a candle behind a piece of red glass for lighting. I also made an enlarger out of a whole plate camera and a biscuit tin, and later my first prints of Barbara won first prize in the beginners' competition at the Bournemouth Camera Club, competing against Leicas, Contaxes and Voigtlanders. This encouraged me to take up photography and I bought a 21/4 inch square Rolleicord for the new price of ten pounds. I went back to old Poole to record people and places that I had known, places that were fast disappearing and local characters that were getting older. In later years Barbara became a professional photographer, and between us, we collected over 750 photographs that eventually became the basis of our photographic history of Poole. People were generous, and we were able to copy old family photographs, pictures of ships, old buildings, maps and the relicts of

Summer wear for men.

Newfoundland traders. We copied old postcards and prints from the early days of photography, items which would otherwise have been lost to posterity. One of the original photographs, 'Summer wear for men', won the gold medal in the Yorkshire Evening News world photographic competition. The collection is now in the possession of Poole Library and about 200 photographs were included in 'A Portfolio of Old Poole', published in 1984.

In 1934 a circus was held at Canford and we travelled the four miles one Saturday afternoon with Barbara who was two years old. The planes were Bristol fighter biplanes, carrying two or three people, and Handley Page bombers converted to passenger planes with twenty four seats. We had never flown before and as it looked quite exciting, we decided to take our first ride for five shillings each in the Bristol fighter. Leaving Barbara with her grandmother, we climbed in to find a small cockpit which came waist high, and three pieces of loose wooden plank on which to sit. A small boy came with us and we could just sit, jammed close together, with the pilot in front of us looking through the propeller. We took off across the bumpy field, climbed to about five hundred feet and circled the field twice. The noise was appalling. We shouted into each others ears without being able to make ourselves heard, and as the plane banked, we hung on to each other because the cockpit seemed to offer no barrier to our falling out, but we certainly had our five shillings worth. Back on the ground, we thought that the Handley Page might be a steadier proposition, the only trouble being the fare of seven and sixpence each. We paid and found two rows of seats, twelve on each side. It was certainly quieter, being totally enclosed and we were able to talk to each other. Once again, we made two circuits of the field but were quite terrified when the plane hit an air pocket and dropped several feet.

Sixty years on, it is difficult to accept that our life-style was accomplished on five pounds a week from my manager's job at the pottery. By now we had our second car, a Singer Le Mans 8.9 horsepower sports model, a real one this time, capable of cruising at 60 m.p.h.. It was bright red with chromium trim, knock-on wheels and four speeds forward for hill climbing, but it had an almost useless hood and side screens. The rear seat would accommodate Barbara, and we were able to use it on summer evenings and weekends. We always went out into the countryside on Saturday afternoons and Sundays, and even used it in the snow.

In 1935, I had an interesting experience. I had borrowed my mother in law's car, a Standard Eight, to go to Bournemouth, and parked in Gervis Place, taking away the key which was simply a tiny piece of flat steel. I did my shopping, returned to the car and drove away through Westover Road, back across the Square and up Poole

Hill. Suddenly, I noticed the model of a policeman standing on the radiator cap and I realised that I was in the wrong car. Turning into the Triangle, I raced across the Square and up Gervis Place to find that my car was still there. I quickly changed over, and before I could start up, a lady came out of a shop and drove away in the car that I had just vacated.

We also maintained an interest in sport. In 1934, we were asked to play in the county badminton trials at Weymouth, and were selected to play as third couple in the first match against Devon at Weymouth. Dorset lost fourteen matches to one, but we beat their fourth couple. For the next few years we played for the Bournemouth club and for the county against Devon, Cornwall and Somerset and later Gloucestershire, travelling by car to St. Austell, Exeter, Bath and Gloucester. We played together at Bournemouth and won the Hampshire Clubs Cup, which Barbara also won in the 1950's.

Travelling in the Singer Le Mans, Dorothy and I were coming back from Exeter to Poole one evening and stopped for a meal in Honiton and for a pint of cider at the village pub. The landlady suggested that the cider might be a bit rough for the lady, but it was the end of a strenuous day and we ignored her advice. Before this, our only experience of cider had been Whiteways bottled preparation and we had found it quite mild. This was Devonshire scrumpy, and within a few miles I was, to say the least, sleepy. Nevertheless, we carried on, until a few miles from Puddletown, we ran out of petrol. I was completely competent. We pushed the car some distance, but on a slope she took off and although I jumped on the running board, Dorothy was left half a mile behind. I managed to stop the car and Dorothy caught up, just as two lads came along. They helped us to push and we arrived at a garage just as the proprietor was locking up. It was eleven o'clock. That was the first and last time that we drank scrumpy. Later four of us used to travel together and we quite often stopped at the Black Bear in Tolpuddle for a drink in the warmth of the tiny bar. We played the farm labourers at darts, always losing, although Dorothy became quite a good player.

By 1938, I had put on weight and had had enough of playing badminton. Being out several evenings a week was affecting our lives. After the All-England match in 1938, the game stopped for most people because of the war, and although I once hoped to play in the All-England Veterans' Championship at fifty, after the war it was too late. By then we had other things to do such as work, palaeontology and rock hunting.

In 1935, I was asked to play cricket for a petroleum company against a local works side in a friendly match at Hamworthy. I was no bowler, but although I had not played seriously for several years, I made a few runs. After the match, the secretary of the works side asked me if I would play for them in the Wareham and District League, to which I agreed. There were about ten teams in the league, mostly from the Purbecks, and the games started at about two o'clock on Saturday afternoons, with most villages using a local farmer's meadow as a pitch. They usually cut the pitches themselves and relied on the cows to keep the outfields reasonably short, keeping them back with iron stakes and a strand of wire. Sometimes the grass could not be cut until hay making, and one village put down a concrete pitch and topped it with matting. Each side brought its own umpire, and the game was usually decided on the first innings, with the winners receiving two points, or one point for a draw.

There was great rivalry between the villages and sometimes the umpiring left much to be desired, but these were minor problems and soon forgotten. In one club the umpire was the father of the fast bowler, and the story went thus. If the ball hit the batsman, no matter where, the cry went up 'How's that, father?', and the reply came back 'Out, my son'. Players turned out in flannels, sometimes with a wide leather belt to support their trousers and a cloth cap. The ex-public school boys were immaculate in whites, and umpires came in their working clothes. Every side had its fast bowler but many players had a chance to bowl. Even I once took three for fourteen. The wives and girl friends provided tea and there was rivalry even in this essential department. Generally speaking, the refreshments were extremely good with home-made cakes and huge kettles of tea, the teams sitting in the wooden shed that constituted the pavilion.

The Dorset dialect dominated some of the games, the broad vowels, the cadence and intonations of the farm labourer bringing joy to the student of language. One fieldsman who was not as diligent as he should have been in chasing the ball was loudly admonished by his captain 'Uncoil thyself thee lazy hound'. We played one match between two Poole teams where tempers flared and the game went completely out of control. We left the field certain that we had won the match, but when our opponents' secretary arrived home, he added up his scorebook and found that it had been totalled wrongly and that his side had won when everyone had agreed that they had lost. It was then found that our scorebook had also been added up wrongly, and in fact the two books did not tally at all. The league warned both clubs as to their future behaviour and awarded them one point each. It cost us the league title, but we won the Knockout Cup, in the final of which I made a duck. These games played in the Purbeck hills were most enjoyable, win or lose. The gently rolling landscape lent beauty to the afternoon, and at the end of the match we made our farewells to the hilltops and looked forward to the next game.

CHAPTER TEN

Our life-style was soon to be severely curtailed, because in 1936 we both caught typhoid fever of a very virulent type by drinking milk supplied by a local dairy. It transpired that a local landowner was a typhoid carrier, unknown to himself, and his cows drank infected water, thereby poisoning their milk. This was before the days of compulsory pasteurisation. A dairy company which supplied about forty shops in Poole, Bournemouth and Christchurch, mixed the milk with that of a large number of other producers and the result was that about one thousand people caught the disease and about forty people died. We were both seriously ill but Barbara, who was four, suffered no ill effects. Dorothy and I were taken into isolation at Alderney on August 2nd 1936 and I did not get back to work until December 10th. Dorothy was very lucky to survive for she was in a coma for several weeks, and we both lost several stones in weight. Alderney Hospital was quite inadequate for the crisis. The men's ward, a wooden hut, had beds for eight men and there were fourteen inmates when I was wheeled in. For about a week, extra huts were hastily erected. Dr. Maule Horne, the Medical Officer of Health, told me later that the epidemic was one of the most virulent known to the medical profession. The dairy became bankrupt and there was no compensation.

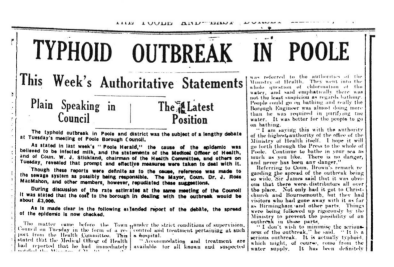

During my absence from work it had been realised that the pottery was vulnerable, as both J. A. and I had been away for long periods. In my absence Ernest Baggaley, a potter from Stoke on Trent, had been engaged to take over the production, which was a great relief to me. He revolutionised the techniques, worked out new glazes, introduced spray glazing instead of dipping, and presided as we took over some more of Carter's space. A complete new factory was again considered, but now war was on the horizon.

The first Nazi flag came to Poole on a ship named the Hinrich Peters, registered in Hamburg. In 1936, she tied up at the main quay, loaded with deals from the Baltic, and her ensign flew from the stern during the whole of her stay. She sailed away light, and rounding Stakes Buoy, she dipped her flag and then raised it as though in derision of the decadent English. By the middle thirties, the happenings in Germany had begun to affect us. Hitler's rise to power brought the Peace Movement into prominence in Britain and a poll was organised which people signed to say that they would not in any circumstances take part in any war. The result was beyond the wildest dreams of the organisers. Britain appeared to be pacifist and a large number of Poole people joined the movement. Later when Neville Chamberlain met Hitler at Berchtesgarten and returned with a promise of 'peace in our time', people in Britain were very relieved, but by the time war actually came to us in 1939, their numbers had all but disappeared.

At this time we usually spent our holidays staying in a cottage or guest house somewhere in the west country, but by the end of the thirties, we felt that it was time to get back to the freedom of doing our own thing by buying a caravan. We realised that the Singer was hardly the best car with which to tow, but we were not in a position to change it. We had exactly £90 to spare and saw an article in 'The Caravan' describing a Curzon caravan made in Bournemouth. I went to see the firm and asked them if they could make me a van for £90, to which they agreed. We specified that it should be ten feet long, made with a single skin of Masonite on an ash frame with a wooden chassis, overrun brakes, one double bed, one single bed and a Tilley lamp for lighting. They started immediately and I went to inspect the progress they made, but then we had a shock because they wrote to say that they wanted another £10 which we would find difficult to raise. I borrowed it from my mother and paid it back at a few shillings a week.

The van was rather heavy in front and we had to trim the balance by travelling with some of the bed cushions over the axle, but the sleeping arrangements were extremely comfortable. We had no great difficulty in towing, and from 1937 to 1939 we travelled the western

A German ship at Poole Quay.

counties of England, until we were no longer able to obtain petrol, when we parked the van at Henbury for the rest of the war. We started caravanning by moving out at midday on Saturdays and returning on Sunday evenings. We explored the Purbeck hills from Corfe Castle to Swanage and Studland, staying at Greenlands, near the mouth of the harbour where we helped with the hay making. We saw the long barrows and round barrows of north Dorset and the iron age hill forts of Badbury Rings and Maiden Castle. At Easter, Whitsun and Bank holidays we set out to explore the Wessex countryside, Wool Manor, associated with Tess of the D'Urbervilles, Bere Regis church, Wimborne Minster with the coffin placed in the wall, the Puddle villages. I also began to collect photographs for my slide lectures.

During the next two years, rumours of war spread throughout Britain. The Graf Zeppelin, the last of its kind, visited Britain in 1938, making a tour of the coastline to test the radar systems. Winston Churchill complained about it in Parliament. It flew over Poole in the mid afternoon, looking very much larger than the ill-fated R101 which I had seen in Bedfordshire in 1930. However, airships were found to be quite unsuited to modern warfare, and after the Hindenburg disaster in Lakehurst, U.S.A., it and its sister ship, Zeppelin 1, were scrapped and the frameworks melted down. At the Gieve's Gallery exhibition in 1938, Stanley Hasted, the pottery's new representative, and I waited for the first German bombs to fall on London, but it was not yet to be. Neville Chamberlain's visit to Munich relieved the situation temporarily. By early July 1939, it seemed inevitable that war was coming and we decided to bring the caravan back to Durdle Door. On that fateful Sunday morning, I took the Singer to collect it. At eleven o'clock, I heard Chamberlain say that we were at war and with very mixed feelings I drove home through the lanes and highways that we had travelled for the last eighteen years. We had named the caravan Persephone because she was stowed away in darkness for the winter and emerged in the spring. Now it seemed as if she would live in eternal darkness, never to reappear.

With the outbreak of war, Poole prepared its defences. The town became a naval base and the main port in England for Sunderland flying boats, a service which continued for most of the war. Two block ships were anchored between Stakes Buoy and Ballast Quay, the Empire Sentinel and *HMS Flinders*, which I photographed through the quayside entrance to the pottery. Troops in convoy passed our house, but in the early months, the war did not make much impact on our lives. Industry was told to carry on as usual and men over thirty were to stay at their jobs, unlike the first World War when thousands of men joined Kitchener's army. Petrol was still available and stories circulated that no one really wanted to fight and that the whole thing would be negotiated for peace.

In the spring of 1940, we took the van out of hibernation back to Greenlands at the mouth of the harbour. We went there at weekends and once again helped with the hay making. One morning our calm was badly shaken when we saw the channel leading to the harbour crowded with fishing boats flying the French flag. They looked neglected and speckled with rust, and their decks were crowded with troops and civilians escaping from the German advance into Brittany. Further north, La Panne, Dunkirk and Calais were being defended to allow the escape of British troops back to England. This gave a breathing space to other areas of France, and these boats were from Roscoff, Cherbourg and Fecamp, with passengers who did not want

Block ships seen from the Quay.

to be subjected to German occupation.

That night we heard the sound of a plane, slow-moving and apparently heavily laden. The engine stopped for about five minutes and then started again, and we heard the sound of machine gun fire followed by silence. When the machine guns started up again, we realised that our masonite caravan gave us no protection at all, but we nevertheless managed to fall asleep. In the morning, we sat on the beach and watched a small patrol boat, an ex-coaster, coming down harbour and making for the English Channel to watch for possible invasion, as there had been rumours of German reconnoitres. It moved peacefully towards the Channel, leaving a wake into which the gulls wheeled and dived, and became a smoky smudge on the horizon. We had lost interest in it when a violent explosion made us look seaward. The ship had disappeared in a cloud of steam and spray. The plane the night before had been German and had laid a floating mine which exploded magnetically as the steel ship passed over it. All the crew perished. More ships were lost until all vessels were routinely degaussed. A metal hawser was welded right round the ship to neutralise the magnetic effect of the mine. After this interlude, we had once more to return Persephone to the darkness.

A harbour patrol was formed under Norman Hibbs, a Parkstone estate agent, with various yachting enthusiasts including Jack Valentine, who became Lieutenant Commander. The *Royal Sovereign*, a London to Margate pleasure steamer, arrived, commanded by Captain Shippick, a Poole man, and sailed the next day. She was huge compared with the local paddle steamers and could have had very little draught to spare. I would have liked to take a shot of her, but did not dare. I was on the Quay in March 1940 when the Pitwines arrived at the gasworks transporter. She had been attacked by a German plane after leaving Hull with a load of coal. I spoke to a member of the crew who said that the only arms they had consisted of one rifle. She showed evidence of machine gun bullets, but sailed away the next day, and as I had photographed her pre-war, I was able to sell a print to the *Bournemouth Echo* for the magnificent sum of seven and sixpence.

At the pottery, we converted a muffle kiln into an air raid shelter and filled sandbags to guard the entrance. When the first siren sounded, we all crowded into the kiln, but four brave lads went out to the Quay to see the German planes coming in. A burst of machine gun fire sent them scuttling back. One day I had to escort two civilians, presumably army officers in mufti, to the factory roof to chose a site for two guns to repel an attack. They agreed that it would be an ideal place for machine guns and small artillery, but Cyril Carter suggested that if they fired the guns, the whole factory would probably collapse. I could only agree. The roof was quite flat and open, and I began to realise the seriousness of the situation. From the warehouse window we could see the small blimps anchored with wire cables to the various vessels to prevent low flying aircraft approaching. I also saw the Poole fishing fleet lined up to help the Dunkirk evacuation. They were led by an armed naval patrol in the Poole lifeboat.

Cyril Carter had commanded one of the Dorset regiments in the Middle East and India during the first World War and he now became Colonel Carter, Officer in charge of Poole Airport. Quite soon after the Sunderland flying boats arrived, he asked me to be at the ferry steps when the next passengers arrived. A suspect was expected to land, and he wanted a photograph of him. A counter spy in the boat would signal by blowing his nose if the man was on board. I was not at all happy, but the C.O. was my peacetime boss, and so I hung around with my Rolleicord. A sailor reported me to his officer for carrying a camera, and I was closely questioned, but I had a signed permission chit and they let me go. Much to my delight, the man did not arrive. There was little chance that I could have photographed him without his knowledge.

The phoney war had come and gone and we had what we thought was a brilliant idea. There was a general fear of invasion, especially as France was so near, and people talked about Germans disguised as monks, nuns and civilians landing at night along the shores of Sandbanks, Studland, and the remoter parts of the harbour. We decided to ask a farmer friend if we could put the caravan on his farm at Sutton Waldron, in North Dorset, about twenty five miles from Poole. He asked his local council and obtained permission, and we moved into a corner of one of his fields. We thereby struck up a friendship which has lasted until now. We had a shock on our first night in the van. We expected bombs in Poole from the returning German planes, but not in what we considered to be an area remote from the war. At midnight, the van was shaken by five explosions. It swayed on its jacks and we realised that we were still in a war zone. A plane on its way back to France had dropped its load on Fontmell Magna, a nearby village, before it reached Poole and the coast. A small post office was destroyed and it was said that one person was killed. In fact the whole of England could expect to be bombed at some time.

At the end of the summer it was obvious that we would not get petrol much longer, and we reluctantly took the van home. That weekend on our way to Sutton Waldron, the countryside had been a hive of activity. Country houses had been commandeered, troops were drilling and army vehicles travelled the Dorset roads, but on that last day, all was quiet. The troops were gone, and we were concerned that invasion was imminent. We expected any time to hear the church bells ringing to announce the start of the German operation 'Sea Lion'. Rumours were running riot. It was said that the bodies of German soldiers had been washed ashore on Chesil Beach, that invasion barges had been sunk off Old Harry Rocks, and that German spies had been dropped by parachute. We approached Poole in trepidation, but it was all a false alarm

The war now came to us in earnest. Goering had promised Hitler that he would drive the R.A.F. from the sky and German planes came across the Channel under the impression that it would be a walk-over. We saw vapour trails without understanding at first what was happening, but we soon discovered their significance. One day we saw a vapour trail disappear and two black objects fall from the sky, one larger than the other. It became clear that they were a plane and a pilot whose parachute had failed to open. The plane was a Spitfire and the pilot came from New Zealand. The road into which he fell was renamed Pilot Hight Road. In 1964, in a caravan park near Kaitaia in New Zealand, we were introduced to a Mr and Mrs Hight who turned out to be his aunt and uncle. I often walked to work because there was no petrol for private cars, and I wondered at times if this would be the day that the German invasion fleet would sail up the harbour. One morning, I found that a large steamer had been sunk close to Poole bridge, a German Heinkel had been shot down and was lying in the mud opposite the pottery, and a Sunderland flying boat had been dragged on to the beach at Ballast Quay. Coming down the High Street one morning at about eight thirty, I saw two soldiers removing some objects from the railway line at the level crossing and taking them into the doorway of Lories furniture shop. Colonel Carter told me later that the objects were land mines that would have been exploded if the Germans had landed. Everyone between the railway lines and the Quay would have been unable to escape, except on foot.

The first bombs to hit Poole came soon after the evacuation from Dunkirk and fell in South Road, Market Place and West Street. The one in Market Place was only the width of the road from the Guildhall and fifty yards from my parents' home. It demolished a second hand shop, killing a woman, and the roads were strewn with nuts and bolts, nails and miscellaneous metal. Rumour had it that the Germans, being short of metal, were filling their bombs with scrap, but this debris came from the shop. My mother 'phoned me in distress and I arrived to find wooden roof beams that had travelled over the house tops, lying in the garden, with pieces of tiles, bricks and masonry. A solid brass door knob had drilled a neat hole in my mother's bedroom window, and was lying on the pillow where an elderly aunt had been sleeping. The Guildhall was apparently undamaged, and we assumed that it could not have been a very large bomb. No details were published, but after the war, we learned that some people in South Road had been killed.

By now every factory was required to send two men to the roof as spotters when the air raid siren sounded. On one of my turns, I saw a German plane coming in, rapidly losing height and with smoke coming from its tail. Something fell from the rear of the plane which I took to be a part of it, but which was actually the rear gunner whose parachute failed to open. He crashed through the roof of Kinson Pottery about three miles away and a few moments later, the plane crashed at Newtown and exploded, killing all the crew. After one raid, I found several bullets that had penetrated the roof and were lying on the floor of the restaurant.

Bomb damage in Poole.

THE POOLE AND EAST DORSET HERALD, WEDNESDAY, JUNE 12, 1940

Founded 189

HAVE AN AIR RAID SHELTER BUILT NOW

Every Householder Should Put Work In Hand

By

HAROLD BUTLER, C.B.

(Southern Regional Commissioner for Civil Defence)

The distinguished author of this article controls the Bournemouth area civil defence and in fact the whole Southern Region. His article, therefore, may be taken as giving the official view that air raid shelters are essential in every home in the Bournemouth Poole area. As such it constitutes a grave warning to all who have not yet provided themselves with this essential protection. While those who are able to do so will naturally seek the advice of the building undertakings on this page (who are in full knowledge of the work), others may yet construct their own shelter quite easily, using the leaflets which give the necessary information and which are available from A.R.P. centres.

MAKE THAT SHELTER NOW!

LESSON OF EXPERIENCE

TWO WAYS OF PROTECTION

YOU CAN HELP!

BUILD HOME DEFENCES

A.R.P. SHELTER SPECIALISTS

Air raid shelters.

CHAPTER ELEVEN

After Dunkirk it was obvious that the production of pottery would become very difficult and it also seemed rather useless in wartime. Already men and women were leaving to join the forces. Marriages became inevitable and collections and presentations in the packing shed became rather too frequent, until J. A. had to call a halt to the ceremony. As the war proceeded, girls left to join the forces and the marriage rate increased. Three paintresses lost their husbands and Richard Damon, a young assistant kiln setter, was lost while serving in the Royal Navy. Some of the staff in their late thirties were transferred to government jobs, as food inspectors in the rationing departments, inspecting sites for airfields and organising scrap metal collections. I began to consider my future. Like a lot of other men no longer young, I was not a warlike type and came from a pacifist background. In fact my father had objected strongly to my becoming a boy scout in the first World War, because of their connection with the Boer War, although this had not deterred me. I applied for a commission in the Royal Air Force as an engineer, but I had been out of the industry for so long that my application was refused. I was told to stay in my job until I was allocated a position more essential to the war effort.

It was obvious that the pottery would at best struggle to survive, and I felt that I could not wait to be directed into a job. For about twelve months a friend of mine had been urging me to manage a small munition works that he had established from a motor repair shop that he owned, but I had turned it down although the financial reward was much greater than my still modest five pounds per week. I was interviewed about my future and the choice narrowed down to Staff Sergeant in the Royal Engineers (goodness knows how they arrived at that one), munitions in Coventry or the friend's job. The army would have been the best, the Coventry job the worst, but in the end I chose the Poole one and lived at home for the rest of the war. I was by no means proud of my war service because I simply let things take their course, but the job was no sinecure. I was appointed to manage three small munitions factories in Newtown and hated every minute of the work I found myself doing. I certainly made no money as, unlike many people I knew, I earned only £12 a week until D-Day; not that it mattered because we could not spend much anyway. We worked shifts, 6.00 until 2.00, 2.00 until 10.00 and 10.00 until 6.00. It was sheer horror, working with little sleep, unable to adjust to the difficult hours and poor working conditions. We used a draughty ex motor repair shop with one coke stove for heating and spent a lot of the time diving under lathes or trucks, wet through with slurry. When I left the pottery, John Adams assured me that my job would be available after the war but it was inevitable that I would lose touch with the pottery while working all day and walking the streets at night as an Air Raid Warden.

The R. A. F. was still battling to contain the daylight raids by fighters and bombers, and there came the great day, a Sunday, when so many German fighters were destroyed that Goering stopped all daylight raids and went over to night bombing. On that Sunday, I was out for a walk across the fields. It was a typical English Sunday afternoon, sunshine, butterflies, the cattle resting under the oaks and beeches, bees collecting pollen, and couples and families strolling to church or Sunday School. Suddenly, there was a roar of aeroplanes, a rattle of machine gun fire and the sound of bullets; some hit a nearby tree. Two planes, one German, one British, skimmed the tree tops and were gone before I could dive to the ground. I watched them and saw the German plane get lower and lower until it glided into a hill two miles away. The Spitfire veered away to the right, climbed steeply, did a complete roll, and sped away. We inspected the German plane later and found that it was undamaged except for a bullet hole through the screen at the back of the pilot's seat.

In 1941, I developed a sharp pain in my left side and a kidney stone was diagnosed. I was hurriedly put into a nursing home and then found myself in Boscombe Hospital. I remember lying on the operating table for observation. The anaesthetist jabbed me with a needle and asked me if I could feel it. I said 'I think so'. He laughed and said that he had 'pushed it in about six inches'. I had an operation. The surgeon had difficulty in finding the stone, but produced a piece of gravel that seemed to have been picked up in the road. I recovered and have had no trouble since, but while I was in hospital, Poole and Bournemouth withstood a major night-time bombing raid by the Luftwaffe. A nurse came in and gave me a papier mache bowl and told me to put it over my head. I tried it but it was so uncomfortable that I put it on the floor and fell asleep, in spite of the noise of bombs and anti-aircraft fire which was deafening. Still feeling the effects of the anaesthetic, I had only a vague idea of what was happening and imagined that what I could see through the window were guns when they were only chimney pots. I only realised the seriousness of the raid when my

The aftermath of the air raid on Bourne Valley Gasworks.

father came to see me, obviously shaken. When the nurse described the ambulances arriving with the injured, it was obvious that this was the most devastating bombing so far. Later it was said that Bourne Valley Gasworks had been hit, and many men killed.

My duties as a warden involved night-time patrols, turning out every night for two years as the bombers came over our house. As soon as darkness fell, which was around 4.30 in the winter, the sirens screamed out, anti-aircraft artillery sent hundreds of shells into the air and shrapnel came hissing down until the planes had passed on to the attack of the West Country and South Wales. The all-clear sounded, only to be replaced by the warning siren when the attackers returned, straggling back out of formation, when we turned out again. There was always the tail-end Charlie who had not dropped all his bombs on Bristol or Cardiff, and dropped them on us because we were the last bit of Britain he saw before crossing back over the Channel. The disturbing whistle of falling shrapnel as it reached the ground made me wonder whether my tin hat would deflect anything that hit it.

There seemed to be rather more than usual one night as I walked up the hill to the wardens' post. The Luftwaffe droned overhead as the anti-aircraft guns blazed away. At the top of Harbour Hill Road, a baldheaded man in his shirt sleeves was leaning over his garden gate, oblivious to the danger and I advised him to go inside. He said that he could hear the shrapnel falling, but had no idea what it was. I arrived at the post at the same time as the three other wardens. We were talking outside when we heard the scream of a falling bomb. It seemed to be exactly overhead, and we all tried to get into the shelter at the same time, finishing in an undignified heap on the pavement. The bomb fell at Whitecliff, at least two miles away. One evening I turned out in full uniform and started to walk up to the post when a terrific noise started, like a large aircraft flying very low and probably in trouble. It sounded so close that I dived for the gutter and lay full length, waiting for it to pass. The noise gradually subsided and I stood up, realising that it was a Sunderland taking off from the harbour some miles away.

One very dark winter's night, a string of five bombs had dropped near Harbour Hill, but only four had exploded. We knew that they were always dropped in a string of five. We four wardens searched tentatively, but there was little that we could do in the dark, even if we had found the unexploded one. We gathered on the edge of a pit, talked for a while, and then moved away to return to base. Suddenly, a violent explosion sent us diving to the ground. After evenings like this, I had to turn out for work to start the 10.00 to 6.00 shift, tool setting, drill grinding and trying to control a group of sixteen to eighteen year old lads, future conscripts and not very interested in what they were doing. Inevitably, the constant disturbance of rest told on my ability to relax. In any case, if I had been five years younger, I could have been killed in a bomber over Germany, or near Cherbourg after D-Day.

The Germans had changed their tactics to attack the civilian populations of major British cities. Southampton, only thirty miles away, was almost completely destroyed, as was its neighbour, Portsmouth, and Plymouth was also subjected to a night of terror. Shortly afterwards, the warning siren sounded at about five o'clock one night, and I turned out and signed on at the wardens' post as the first plane came in very low. It dropped a string of incendiaries about a mile away, which were extinguished just as a fire began to light up the sky away to the south west. The second plane turned and dropped five bombs on the second fire. I was alone, as my warden partner had not arrived, and I went home to stand in the shelter of my front porch, just as the main flight of bombers made their approach. It was worrying because for the first time, the raid was obviously for us. They came in singly, very low, turned over our house and made for the fire which grew in intensity, silhouetting each plane as it came out of the darkness into the glow. About twenty planes had passed over, and the fire spread as the bombs dropped in an ever widening circle. Dorothy and Barbara came out into the porch to see a couple of planes pass, when there was a roar as Spitfires moved into the attack. They retreated to the Morrison shelter erected in the dining room. The raid continued as about fifty planes came in, and then suddenly the all-clear sounded and it was over. People came out to discuss why the town had escaped destruction. No official explanation was ever offered, but the next day a fire was still burning at the north end of Brownsea Island, and the opinion was that the Pathfinder incendiaries had been extinguished and a decoy fire had been lit on Brownsea.

In the midst of these difficult times, we still managed to get away to the countryside occasionally. A friend told us of some woodland that was for sale about ten miles from Poole at Henbury near Sturminster Marshall. Henbury House, an Elizabethan manor, had been sold, and a developer had divided up the surrounding estate into blocks of one or two acres. My friend had bought one block for £30 and he knew of several buyers who would sell at a modest profit. We bought about two acres. It was heavily wooded with oak, beech and silver birch trees, with rhododendron ponticum covering the ground between them. The rhododendrons had been there for several hundred years and some had trunks about a foot in diameter. Parts of the land were impassable because of them. When in flower, they were

Air raid damage, Poole.

a mass of purple glory, and to us, coming from a town under siege, unpalatable labour and sleepless nights, it was a garden of peace.

Here we revelled in an entirely new way of life. The plot rose to the edge of a plateau from which we could see Badbury Rings, the historic earthworks, several miles away. We also had a pond where mallards came. Gradually, we began to clear the ground. We cleared a well, cleaning out the mud of past generations and installing concrete pipes. We then bought a plot each for Barbara, my mother and Dorothy's mother and extended our area so that we now owned a country estate at a very low cost. It was by any standards very rough. We had road access, but it was rather difficult in wet weather. Spring came early to Henbury and sometimes we were able to cycle the ten miles and sleep there in the small caravan. Gradually we came to appreciate its beauty. Wood pigeons roosted in the tall beeches and woke us early in the morning, cooing contentedly, while rabbits fed in the nearby meadow. To our regret, our visits were infrequent that spring. Britain was besieged, bombs were falling and we were needed at home.

Petrol was now unavailable for private use. Some could be obtained for essential travel from place to place along a definite route but anyone caught abusing the terms of the permit was heavily fined. We were refused any petrol at all and so went back to bicycles. At Henbury we cleared a level patch of ground of bracken, dug it all out with a spade, and grew a ton of potatoes, King Edwards and Red Kings. They were huge because of the hundred or so years of leaf mould on the ground, not to mention the bracken which we burnt for potash. We had a slight problem with the odd dormouse and tiny rabbits who could squeeze through the smallest wire mesh. We sometimes found a dormouse hibernating in his nest of hay. Our trees were home to woodpeckers, jays, nuthatches and pigeons and as a change from rabbit, I shot a pigeon or two. We also had grass snakes, adders and slow worms. Barbara, now ten years old, enjoyed herself making elderberry or wild strawberry jam on a Milboro stove.

Unexpectedly we now found a new source of income. We cut down sapling sycamores and sold them as bean rods, and dug up the leaf mould, which was several feet thick, sifted it, and sold it to greengrocers shops. The return was quite small, but then we had never been rich and everything helped. We began to cut firewood by hand using bow saws, and found that wood was in great demand. As we sold it by the sack to neighbours, transport became a problem. My father had a Commer one ton van, (his two other trucks having been taken over by the Fire Brigade). His petrol was rationed and the use of the vehicle had to be declared with the mileage recorded. We declared him to be a firewood merchant, obtained a petrol allowance,

'The bend in the road'. Henbury in the snow.

and thereafter faithfully recorded the journeys on log sheets. My father, mother, Dorothy, Barbara and I rode on the truck to Henbury, usually on a Sunday, loaded as much firewood as possible, and took it back to the yard where the van was garaged. One Sunday it started to rain on the way back. I had dropped my parents at their house, and Dorothy and Barbara were sitting on the wood, high in the top of the van. I had stopped outside our house to drop them off and to take in several sacks of firewood, when an inspector arrived and asked me to explain what I was doing. I assured him that I was a firewood merchant and that he would find the records correct, but kept Dorothy and Barbara in the van until he had gone. We were never again stopped.

Henbury gave us five years of pure pleasure, in spite of the hard work. We did not make any money, but sold enough firewood to pay back the £300 that the first ten acres cost us. I planted a walnut tree for future generations and put an engraved plate on it 'PLANTED BY ERNEST BRISTOWE - 1942', and also planted thirty conkers which grew into beautiful horse chestnut trees. We cleared large areas of rhododendron with bow and crosscut saws and by hauling on ropes, but by the time we had cleared a patch, the previous one had regrown. After the war, we sold our holding for £300, the original cost price. My mother, Dorothy's mother and Barbara kept theirs and finally sold them for £150 an acre. Goodness knows what it is like today; probably developed into country estates at fabulous prices. Above all, the activities at Henbury gave us something different and helped to bring us through the war.

In spite of the war, the Poole fishing fleet carried on, at least with the sprat harvest. Before the war, sprats had been unsaleable, but now it was said that some boats were earning £1000 a week. The fish still shoaled in Poole Bay outside the harbour immediately after Christmas, usually on Boxing Day, and Britain was so short of food that we would eat anything. Clothing coupons were a nightmare. My suit was about ten years old, but as I never had the opportunity to wear it, this really did not matter. Barbara, however, was growing rapidly, and it took all our three lots of coupons just to clothe her. In the last year of the war, after five years of clothes rationing, we were almost without anything wearable at all. Dorothy had an aunt who was a dressmaker and she made us two overcoats from army blankets. They were dyed blue and cost 12/6 each, and we wore them for several years. Women wore underwear made from silk parachute panels. The people of Poole collected scrap, even tins, and nothing was wasted. Old tramway lines, buried for years, were ripped up. A Russian cannon, captured at Sebastopol, once had pride of place in Poole Park where small boys climbed onto its barrel, threw stones into its muzzle and polished the eagle that adorned it. Some time before the war, it had been removed to Sterte looking out over Holes Bay. Now it disappeared, together with the bronze drinking fountain that stood outside the Drum Druid in Longfleet Road. Presumably they went for scrap to help the war effort like the railings from the park and from some of Poole's houses and mansions. The whole town was scoured for any metal that could be spared. Aluminium kitchen utensils were collected, housewives giving them willingly to be made into Spitfires and Hurricanes. The rate of destruction later in the war made it improbable that this kind of sacrifice was a great help, but it did boost morale.

The Luftwaffe had ignored Poole and Bournemouth for a considerable time, but in 1943, my mother had a frightening experience when sitting in a deck chair on the sea front at Bournemouth. Suddenly, three planes came in nearly at sea level, climbed over the pier, dropped a string of bombs each, banked steeply and turned for France. My mother, no expert in plane recognition, realised that they were enemy planes when she saw the black crosses on one that passed directly over her. A large number of people was killed, including service men billeted in the Metropole Hotel, although this was only a rumour at the time. No official

Barbed wire, Sandbanks.

account was issued. The next day, we saw machine gunners placed in the gardens alongside the Bourne Stream. The incident was one of the surprise raids that were carried out against many towns along the south coast just to show that the Luftwaffe was still operating.

Around the same time it was decided to hold a mock raid on Poole by a company of commandos. All groups of Civil Defence were alerted, wardens, first aid and W.V.S. With another warden, I was to patrol from the Warden's Post in Dorchester Road to Longfleet Church where the W.V.S. had a refreshment stall. What we were supposed to do was not at all clear. We had reached St. Mary's Road when an army officer appeared out of hiding, pointed a revolver at my stomach, and shouted 'Halt'. I was not exactly pleased. He questioned us to make sure that we were not the enemy in disguise, but eventually let us go with the comment 'Off you go. You look nice in your helmets', obviously not impressed that we contributed much to the war effort. We arrived at the refreshment stall and were given a bun and a cup of tea, when two black-faced commandos came round the corner, tommy guns at the ready. They looked at us in surprise, with no idea what to do about us, and eventually turned and ran. Presumably if the raid had been the real thing, we would have all been shot, but in those circumstances, it is doubtful whether we would have been there, drinking tea and eating buns - C'est la guerre.

We battled on. Hitler's attack on Russia brought relief from bombing which was reduced to small hit and run raids by two or three planes. By 1944, things had improved for me. Shift work was scrapped and work sessions changed to 8.00 am to 12 noon and 1.00 pm. to 5.00 pm. Instead of boys, we had older ladies who wanted to win the war, and girls and married women with families. They worked only a four hour shift and production increased dramatically. Civil Defence became a comparatively interesting activity, except that the Germans had now put a bomb in the tail of their incendiaries, making them dangerous and frightening. A friend of mine in Civil Defence was killed by one on Poole Quay.

We civilians had no idea that summer that the invasion was imminent, although Poole Bay was full of ships of all shapes and sizes. Transport had been pouring along the roads on the outskirts of town, and once I had been unable to get home from the works at 5.00 because of about a hundred tanks coming down the main highway from the north, presumably on their way to Weymouth. I waited over an hour for them to pass, too scared to mount my bicycle. All this activity and preparation went along without any interference from the Germans. On June 6th 1944, we were awakened by the continuous roar of heavy bombers. We hurried out to see one of the most spectacular events of the war. The sky was full of American Flying Fortresses, Halifaxes and Albermarks, each towing a black, sinister looking glider. They flew in formation, low over the houses, heading for the English Channel. The invasion of France had obviously begun. The bombers had sixty miles to go to the landing beaches, and we knew that they would be back. At about midday, they began to return, a few in formation, but mostly in twos and threes and all without the gliders which had landed in France. They were so low that we could see those that had been pitted with gunfire. Two were burning and we hoped that they would make it back to Tarrant Rushton airfield, twelve miles away, near which Persephone was parked in the rhododendrons. Eventually, the last one limped in, with one engine on fire, making for Tarrant Rushton.

Our life went on in the same pattern, but this was the beginning of the end of the war. From Henbury we had seen dogfights between Spitfires and Messerschmidts over our plateau. We had seen Flying Fortress bombers and gliders, some in their hundreds and others alone, flying bravely towards France and returning wearily and sometimes on fire. Occasionally, a lone German plane came over flying high, a mere speck among the cumulus clouds, with anti-aircraft guns opening fire although way off target. We remembered them all when we lit our bonfire on VE Day, on the tip of the plateau in the quiet of an English evening. There were no sounds of war, planes, bombs or anti-aircraft fire. We heard the crackle of our rhododendron branches, and as the fire slowly faded, the sound of the evening breeze in the oaks and silver birches.

In the evening, we went to Bournemouth, where thousands of people gathered in Westover Road outside the cinema, shouting, cheering and dancing in the street. Lights flooded the buildings and everyone was deliriously happy. In the cinema, Ronald Brickell played his Wurlitzer organ, the sound broadcast to the streets and audible several miles away. We sang 'Land of Hope and Glory', all the Vera Lynn wartime songs, 'I'll See You Again' and even 'Tipperary'. Peace had returned. No more fear of invasion, no more blackout, no more bombs or vapour trails in the sky. We would return to normal family life, those of us who had survived. We would be able to travel again, and rationing would cease.

Victory celebrations, Harbour Hill Road, 1945.

Flying boat laid up at Hamworthy

CHAPTER TWELVE

One sign of the peace was the return of the Breton onion men from Roscoff. Louis, Paul and Francois had all survived the German occupation and now reappeared, older but still persistent, wooden pole on shoulder, carrying double strings of onions, arguing, pleading at back doors, refusing to go, lowering the price until in sheer desperation the householder gave in and bought a string. The trouble was that they would return long before the onions had been eaten.

A crisis now arose for me. Should I stay in engineering or go back to the pottery. I had discussed returning to C.S.A. with John Adams, but I met Ernest Baggaley who told me that he had handed in his resignation. He felt that he had brought the pottery through the war, working at every process and even stoking the boiler. The war had affected the pottery very badly with a rapid decline of orders and the threat of destruction of the works. Ernest Baggaley had asked for a directorship but this was refused. He then resigned, but this was also refused, so he applied to the tribunal for his release. He and J. A. appeared before the tribunal which upheld his application, and he was allowed to resign. I later met J. A. and his version of events was entirely different. When he left the tribunal, he was under the impression that he had succeeded, and was very surprised to find that Ernest Baggaley had continued his application, which was then granted.

After leaving C.S.A., Ernest Baggaley opened a pottery at Westbourne in a disused bake house, using town gas for firing. He met a Mr. Sweeney, who by sheer coincidence I had met during the war when he was a manufacturer of aircraft parts, and they opened a new factory, Branksome Ceramics Ltd., making teaware. For the first time C.S.A. had competition, and J. A. was not pleased. The trouble was that when Ernest Baggaley left, he took with him the Glaze Recipe Book. He told me, I think with some justification, that it was he who had developed the glazes, and that they were his property. John Adams, however, contended, also with some justification, that the glazes had been developed by an employee in the company's time, and that they therefore belonged to C.S.A.. The issue was never resolved and Branksome continued to use the glazes.

Poole High Street and South Road, 1960.

The position at C.S.A. was changing rapidly. Harold and Phoebe Stabler had passed away. After Ernest Baggaley left, new directors were appointed and John Adams relinquished control, to concentrate on his design and experimental work in the studio. I realised that the C.S.A. that I had known was disappearing. I now faced a crisis. Should I stay in engineering or go back to the pottery? In either case, the money would only be £10 or £12 per week and I was tired of working for other people. The alternative was to revive the family haulage business which would please my mother as she had always been opposed to my doing manual work.

The business had been started by my grandfather Bristowe who opened a grocer's shop in Poole in 1856, and as the owner of a horse and cart, became the local carrier. My father, being the youngest son, stayed at home to help, as was usual, and inherited what by 1910 was a small but prosperous business. The grocer's shop was abandoned and another horse and cart introduced. By 1923, my father owned three one ton trucks which eventually became one van, a Commer, and two two-ton Bedfords. At the outbreak of war, the two trucks were taken over by the fire brigade at a pittance, and for the rest of the war, the business deteriorated considerably. The two trucks came back in shocking condition, and when the war ended, the value of the business was probably nil. I was still in engineering, and managed to get one truck into reasonable condition. I found that work was available carrying Italian prisoners of war who had been captured in Africa and were now clearing up the mess caused by German bombing. There was not much wear and tear on the vehicle and the job consisted mainly of waiting around to take the men back to their billets. Furthermore, it paid. I then put the other vehicle back on the road and sent it to London on the same kind of work. The money was not exceptional, but it was obviously better than the £10 or £12 a week that seemed to be facing me.

Dorothy and I discussed the situation. We were forty three years old, rather late to start what would probably be hard physical work. We decided to go ahead, and it turned out to be about ten times harder than we ever expected. It took us fifteen years; for me, hard physical toil, for Dorothy, running the house, looking after Barbara, and endless bookkeeping in the evenings. At first, we took £8 a week wages. By the sheerest luck, we decided to phase out haulage and become furniture removers. As it happened, we could not have made a better decision because the next Labour Government nationalised transport, but omitted furniture removers as being a special industry. There were one or two anxious moments as we had to prove that the business had always had some removal operations. However, we made it and became Bristowes Removals Limited. We converted the Commer into a small furniture van and brought back one of the two-tonners. On this I welded a series of iron hoops, put a canvas sheet over it and called it a furniture van. We left the truck with the prisoners of war. Ten years later, we owned six large furniture pantechnicons which travelled the whole of Great Britain. We rented a 10,000 square feet warehouse and a disused school as a furniture store, as well as four other stores, and handled the whole of the furniture intake of the Winfrith Atomic Energy Commission for three years.

For the first few years our lives became simply a matter of being up no later than seven in the morning and of going to bed dead tired. A removal could start at seven o'clock, and by eight o'clock at night, we would still be trying to finish it off. From the beginning, I felt that a large number of jobs needed my personal attention, and I found myself carrying pianos, uprights and grands, up and down stairs, sometimes several flights. There were recurring problems. Britain had lost thousands of homes by bombing. Wealthy people found themselves unable to maintain large houses, which were sold and often divided up into flats. A five storey Victorian mansion in Bournemouth could house eight to ten families and the only way to install the furniture was for two or three men to carry it all up.

Another problem was with people moving from large houses into smaller accommodation. The furniture simply would not get past the banisters and the low headroom of the new council houses which were being erected all over Britain, and of course, we did not know in advance what the house at the other end would be like. People decided that they wanted to live in the country, and thatched cottages and village pubs were a nightmare. We became experts at removing windows, dragging wardrobes up ladders, and turning pianos on end to get them over the banisters at the top of the stairway.

In the evenings, if I was still awake, we had invoices to type, quotations to make, wages, log sheets, time sheets and receipts to organise. Around 1953, we established an office away from the house, engaged some staff, and managed to relax somewhat, and in 1955, took our first long holiday for ten years. We had taken the odd weekend off caravanning, chiefly at rallies of the Caravan Club, Southern Section, and had been as far as Cornwall for a few days. Our small caravan had cost us £100 in the 1930's. In 1946, we sold it and bought a Rollalong for about £400. We traded the Singer in for a monstrous 20 H. P. Armstrong Siddeley saloon. It looked magnificent but was a disaster. We spent money on it but to no avail and in the end we dumped it for £100, and went over to a Landrover. We saw a great deal of Britain by caravan. At weekends we travelled Dorset, Devon, Hampshire and Somerset. Longer weekends saw us further afield. Easter, Whitsun and August Bank Holiday meant that we could travel as far as the Midlands, to Cornwall, Gloucestershire and Sussex. We were now well equipped with the Landrover and decided to take some longer holidays, first to Wales and Scotland, and then, as we became more adventurous, to Belgium, France, Germany and Italy.

Dorothy and I had been interested in photography for some time, and had always processed our own films and prints. When Barbara was born in 1932, we began to take the hobby seriously. With a new Rolleicord, we joined the Bournemouth Camera Club, attended lectures, and entered the various competitions. After a year or so, we began to record the history of Poole and to photograph the Dorset coastline. I became a member of the Society of Poole Men and gave my first lecture to them in 1945 on the subject of 'Poole, its Harbour and its History'. At the end, the secretary of the Workers' Educational Association asked me if I would care to lecture on its behalf to village organisations in East Dorset, and he offered me the magnificent sum of one guinea per lecture. Having agreed, I enlarged my repertoire, and for the next ten years, talked almost every week to church and social groups, Country Women's Associations and Women's Institutes. The demand grew, and I went further afield into Dorset and Hampshire and extended my venues and subjects to include camera clubs and nature study.

Lecturing at the Walton-on-Thames Camera Club, I was asked if I would like to join the Nature Photographic Society of England, and so began ten years of work which was scrutinised by some of the best nature workers in the country. We each contributed twelve photographs a year, and two folders were circulated to each member, one containing a new photograph for comment, and the other containing a previous entry with the comments of each member. I specialised in wild flowers, flying gulls and zoo animals, and from my successes over ten years' membership, I made application for the Associateship of the Royal Photographic Society of England of which I had been a member for many years. I submitted twelve of my best nature photographs, enlarged to 12" by 15". I listed the lectures to camera clubs, my presidency of the Bournemouth Camera Club and my years of working in Britain and Europe. To my delight, I was accepted for Associateship, a prized achievement among amateur and professional photographers.

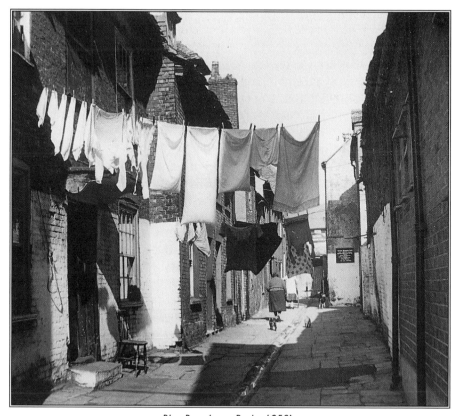

Blue Boar Lane, Poole, 1950's.

New flats at Sterte, 1962.

In 1950, I entered some photographs in the Bournemouth Camera Club's International Exhibition, and one entry of nine children leaning over Poole Quay attracted the attention of the editor of the *Poole and East Dorset Herald*. He published it and we offered to give a photograph to any child who recognised him or herself. We had twelve applications, and all received a photograph. The picture is now in the collection in Poole Reference Library and was published in '*A Portfolio of Old Poole*'. This was the start of an association with the paper that lasted for five years. Every week, I produced a Dorset study for the front page and this involved travelling through the county at every opportunity. Thus I gained an extensive knowledge of its history and geography which helped to establish my lectures. I was also able to record some of the old steets and buildings of Poole before they were demolished, old courts and alleys making way for new high-rise blocks.

I had also been working as a freelance photographer for various national and local papers, and during this period, I recorded a trip for English Life Publications with Arthur Browse who came to Poole from Torquay to establish a crab and lobster fishery. He brought a ten ton Torbay crabber and opened premises in East Street as well as a stall on the Quay. Our acquaintance began when I bought a crab from him and he bought one of my paintings from an exhibition on the Quay.

He invited me to take a trip on the boat to collect the pots off St. Alban's Head. We left Fisherman's Dock at six o'clock one morning with Pat Matthews and another crewman, and made for Old Harry Rocks where we turned to starboard. Off St. Alban's Head, we turned south for a few miles to pick up the marker flags of the pots that had been laid two days before. I was surprised that we were so far away from land because I remembered Jim Harvey catching lobsters off Sandbanks before the first World War. However there was no doubt that this was a good fishing ground. Crabs and lobsters were found in

Arthur Browse, 1950.

every pot, which was then rebaited and cast overboard. Arthur Browse continued fishing for about another five years before he gave up because the grounds were over-fished. He also established a bottled mussel trade, and sold them from his stall with crabs, lobsters, cockles and whelks. I was sorry to see him go, for a Poole hen crab is the finest of edible crustaceans.

Another chance to take photographs came when I went out with Jimmy James, the senior Poole pilot, to guide in one of the tankers that brought petrol to Poole from the Southampton refineries. The

The 'Esso Tioga' entering Poole Harbour, 1949.

Esso Tioga was waiting off Bar Buoy by Old Harry Rocks, and we climbed on board to be introduced to Captain Abrahams. We followed the Shell Bay shoreline to the Haven, and the Captain sounded the siren to warn the ferry of our approach. Then we came up the main channel to off load at several depots. I learned later that the captain of the ship had reported to the company that a cameraman had boarded the ship at Old Harry. The company was worried that I would record the fact that everyone received the same basic petrol, although they mixed in their own additives. In fact I did not reveal that three different petrol companies were getting the same brew. I was very pleased with the results of the photography which looked well in the *Dorset Countryside* magazine.

When the removal business was well established, and we could get away for an odd weekend, we found a caravan site at Ringstead Bay, a few miles east of Weymouth. There were only twelve vans there, and we and a friend made up the number to fourteen. At every opportunity, we spent the weekend there. It proved to be one of the best locations we had ever used. Walking along the beach one morning, I found a beautiful fossil, subsequently identified as Pleurotomaria, and alongside it, a fossilised cockle, Rhynchonella Inconstans, and I had discovered a wonderful new hobby. Ringstead is in the middle of the Jurassic System which stretches along the whole Dorset coast from Old Harry Rocks to Lyme Regis, and provides some of the best exposures in the world. Fossil hunting became my main hobby.

West Bay the sea outlet for Bridport was originally a seaport with a small fishing fleet where wooden sailing coasters were built. Its tiny harbour was protected by two stone piers with an entrance channel between them. Small ships brought timber from the Baltic, and the trade still existed in the 1930's. The ships could only enter the harbour on a high tide and even then, could bump themselves over the small sand bars. The general use of the harbour was for private fishing boats and sea bathing, and it became a holiday resort. We found West Bay to be a very pleasant place for a caravan holiday or a long weekend at Easter or Whitsun. The caravan park bordered the road along the sea front and it gave us a wide, sandy beach. Its small harbour made a safe anchorage for small motor boats and yachts.

I once caught a two pound sea bass from the pier and used its head in a ringnet as bait. Barbara and I caught 420 prawns that night, staying out until midnight, and cooking them on our Milboro paraffin stove. We also caught mackerel, a fine, edible fish, easily caught around the coasts of Britain. In Weymouth Bay and other sites along the Dorset, Devon and Cornish coasts, the fish shoals in fantastic numbers. Weymouth in the 1920's was known as a mackerel town.

At a Dorset Senior Cup Final, Weymouth against Bournemouth Gasworks at Dorchester, the Weymouth supporters arrived with long canes, each with a mackerel tied to one end with white and blue ribbons. Weymouth lost, one nil, and tempers frayed. By the end of the match, the mackerel had deteriorated considerably.

In 1953, we went to London to Winston Churchill's first painting exhibition at the Royal Academy, and I decided to take up painting as a hobby. At school in 1918, I had been reasonably good at drawing, probably better than the chap I sat next to, and I had been indentured as an engineering draughtsman, but I had no experience of oils and had not practised any free-hand drawing for about thirty years. I bought a box of paints which had twenty four colours, a palette and two small canvasses. That summer, we spent a few days holiday at Mevagissey and I sat on the quayside painting the fishing boats without very much idea about procedure. I was encouraged by a gentleman who was obviously an artist. He wore a red shirt, yellow tie and brown corduroy trousers, sported a ginger beard and carried a bundle of drawings. Looking at my efforts, he said 'Jolly good'. I replied that I could not paint, but he said 'My dear Sir, you can draw'. I therefore kept trying, and I have now been painting for thirty years with a great deal of pleasure. I joined the Poole and East Dorset Art Society which had its first exhibition at the fish market on Poole Quay, and I sold my first painting for the magnificent sum of three guineas framed. It showed a collier unloading at the gasworks transporter and it was bought by Arthur Browse, the lobster fisherman. This exhibition was the forerunner of many held in various locations, with the Society's annual exhibition held in the great hall of Parkstone School, and I showed regularly with moderate success.

Our life in the winter consisted of working for five or even six days a week, sometimes twelve hours a day, but we managed to be free sometimes on Saturday afternoons to go to steeplechase or point to point meetings. A visit to Newton Abbot steeplechase while on holiday had given us a liking for the sport of kings. Wincanton was only forty miles away and the Portman and South West Wilts hunts held their annual point to point steeplechases within a few miles of Poole. The Isle of Wight hunt held their meeting on the mainland, and the New Forest Foxhounds also held an annual event. They were all run in the winter season and that usually meant heavy coats, warm hats and Wellington boots. The Portman hunt was held at Badbury Rings and we three became regular fans. The going was frequently soft and it was a tough course for amateur huntsmen. Falls and disasters were frequent and we found the courage of the women to be incredible. They rode the same course as the men with formidable brushwood fences, the plain ones five or six feet high and very wide, as well as post and rail and water jumps. It was also tough on the horses.

I found that panning with my Rolleiflex I could obtain some dramatic photographs of horses clearing the jumps, and I became friendly with riders and owners. I had a number of acceptances from the national paper *Horse and Hound*. I usually operated four or five fences from the start and one day at Badbury Rings I had a shock as five women riders fell at the fence near which I was kneeling. Women and horses were spread all over the ground. As a Boy Scout I had learnt first aid, but five women in breeches, silks and hard hats were beyond my capability. I was imagining broken collar bones or even broken legs, but thank goodness they all recovered enough to walk back to the dressing room. On one occasion I was fortunate not to be seriously injured when I was kneeling close to a fence to take photographs and a horse crashed through the side of the fence on landing. A hoof hit the camera against my ribs but I was falling away instinctively and was able to walk back to the stands.

1964 was a busy year for us. The previous year, Barbara left England to go to New Zealand and after six months of indecision, we decided to follow her. The business was now successful and our trips abroad with the caravan had given us a taste for exploring different countries. We were planning to sail in August and were taking the Landrover, Carousel caravan and about one ton of chattels, which chiefly belonged to Barbara. We decided early in the year to visit the places that we had seen over the last half century, taking in the West Country, Wales and Scotland.

Plans for the journey then had to be finalised, but we found that a passage was almost impossible to book. In fact some agents were suggesting a two year delay. We heard of two Dutch ships which were to be converted for passengers, but no one knew when, and of another ship that rolled so badly that she needed stabilisers. Even the great Thomas Cook could not help. Our names were 'on the list' which seemed to mean very little. I read all that I could find about New Zealand and learned that Shaw Savill was the shipping company which had founded the trade between the Land of the Long White Cloud and Britain in the days of sail. In desperation, I walked into my travel agent's office and said 'Have you tried Shaw Savill? Ring them'. He rang and the conversation went: 'Can you take two people to New Zealand?' Pause. 'You can? When? August the thirteenth?' I shouted 'Book it' He waved me down. 'First class.' I shouted 'Book it' He booked it. I said 'Ask them if they can take a caravan and Landrover.' 'You can? Book it.' We were booked on the *S.S. Gothic*. We received a letter to confirm the booking but they said that we were not to use the caravan as a packing case. We explained that we needed to take enough for us to live in it for a year or two and they agreed and also allowed us to take about one ton of chattels which were packed in four wooden cases. We filled the lockers of the caravan, screwed them down, and sat back to await the fateful day. We were now nearing the date of departure and held a farewell dinner at the Station Hotel, Bournemouth Central with the four friends who had dined with us at Cavallino. Together we relived our caravan days.

The gravity of the decision we had made gradually dawned on us. The company, Barbara's photographic business, our friends and our association with Poole were to be completely abandoned. We were sixty one, at an age when most rational people were thinking of sitting back and resting, but we were the impulsive ones, starting all over again. VIGILANTIBUS NON DORMIENTIBUS was our new motto. We sold the house and the various holdings we had acquired. The company we left to run with new directors, and we left our money in England as the rate was greatly in our favour and we were concerned that we might find ourselves with insufficient capital and unable to find work. We might even return to Poole, but here was an adventure more thrilling than our first European journey, and if we could not afford a house, then we would live in the caravan.

As the sailing date drew near, we relaxed and began to look forward to crossing the Atlantic and then the Pacific, landing in the West Indies and passing through the Panama Canal. We bought books about New Zealand and saw photographs of lovely Maori girls in grass skirts, the snow clad peaks of Mount Cook, the thousands of sheep on the Canterbury Plains, and the hot springs and geysers of Rotorua. We went to New Zealand House in London to get information, and came away enthralled by the prospect of the warmth of the country and the wide open spaces. On a negative note we were subdued to meet a couple on Poole Quay who had gone to New Zealand to be with their family, but hated every minute of it and had returned. However we were committed and were determined to make it work.

On August 7th 1964, we left Poole at eleven o'clock in the evening for London, our four boxes of chattels having been sent on ahead to the Royal Albert Dock. The Landrover and caravan had to be at King George V Dock a week before sailing. We drove along Oxford Street at three o'clock in the morning to avoid the London traffic but even at that time there was a diversion sign due to road-works, and as usual, we got completely lost and had to go back to Marble Arch to start again. A policeman looked at us in amazement as we passed him for the second time and I felt that I must get the route right or I would find myself in the police station helping him with his enquiries. After all, who would be caravanning twice round

Marble Arch at three o'clock in the morning? Eventually, we found the docks and pulled off the road on to a bomb site outside the dock gates. At six o'clock, a friendly docker advised us to get lined up at the dock gates, otherwise we would be hemmed in. 'Every docker has a car.' he said. We left our vehicles in the dock shed and took a taxi to a hotel in the Haymarket with a week to wait and sight-see in London.

The S. S. *Gothic* left the Thames just after midnight on August 14th and from the portholes of the cabin we watched the warehouses dimly lit with an occasional street light and the barges, tugboats and coastal freighters silhouetted against the starlit sky. We slept, and after breakfast, when the pilot left us, everyone came up on deck to see the white cliffs for the last time. Little did we realise it; we were bound not only for New Zealand but we could have sung: 'Now all you young lads and lasses / Just listen to what I do say / Sing Tooruli ooruli addity / We're bound for Botany Bay.'

Ernest, Dorothy and Barbara.

INDEX

A

Adams, John   79-80, 84, 86, 98,
                   107-108, 119-120.
, Neild   80, 83-84.
, Truda   82-83, 86.
Air raid wardens 108-110, 115-116.
Alderney Hospital   97.
Antelope Hall   76.
Arne   29, 73, 89.
Arnold, Bobby   29.

B

Badbury Rings   12, 99, 112, 128.
Baden-Powell, Lord   58.
Badminton   76, 95.
Baggaley, Ernest   87, 98, 119-120.
Bailey, Mr.   34.
Baiter   37.
Ballast Quay   24, 70, 100, 104.
Bartletts'   60.
Baverstocks'   36.
Beating of the Bounds   73.
Bere Regis   99.
Bethel Mission   33.
Betts, Granny   36.
Bibby, Beatrice   88.
Bicycles   44-45, 55, 60, 89.
Bishton, Harry   88.
Blacksmith   44.
Blues, Bobby   9, 42.
Boone and Gibletts   46.

Bourne Valley Gasworks   109.
Bournemouth Camera Club   122-4.
  Central Station   42.
  Echo   102.
  Gas and Water Company   31.
  Square   73, 94-95.
Boy Scouts   17-18, 47, 57-58, 60.
Bradbury, Arthur   87.
Branksome Band   60.
Branksome Ceramics Ltd.   119.
Branksome Park   52
Branksome Railway Station   41.
Breakheart Lane   65.
Brickell, Ronald   117.
Brighton   72-73.
Bristowe, Barbara   80, 91-94,
                      97, 122, 129.
, Dorothy   10, 71-80, 85-86,
              91-93, 95, 97,
              121-122.
Bristowes Removals Ltd.   121-122.
Brown Bottom   41, 59.
Brown, Lily   86.
Brownsea Island   19, 22, 29, 47,
                   57, 73, 111.
Browse, Arthur   124-126. 128.
Bryant, William   80.
Buckle, Mr.   46.
Burden, Henry   55.
Burdens' Chandlers   22, 26.
Burge, Steve   60.

C

Camping   51, 90-91.
Canford   94.
Canford Cliffs   52.
Caravanning   98-103, 112, 122, 127, 129.
Carnival   59-60.
Cars   44, 78, 90-91, 94-95.
Carter, Cyril   79, 86, 102, 104.
  , Herbert   14.
  , Owen   79, 83.
Carters' Almshouses   88.
Carter, Stabler and Adams   22, 24, 79-88, 98, 102, 107, 119-120.
Central Hotel   71, 76.
Cherbourg   70.
Chislett, Mr.   25.
Christopher Hill   44.
Christopher, Mr.   44.
Cinema   48, 62-64.
Clay   22.
Cleaver, Mr.   17.
Co-operative Society   36.
Coal   22-24, 31, 37.
Coastlines   18.
Cole, Henry   45, 50.
Cole, Mr.   46.
Conkers   64-65.
Constitution Hill   19, 73-74.
Conway, Mr.   19, 31.
Corfe Castle   89, 99.
Cornelia Hospital   47.
Cornibeer, Harold   65.
Cousins, Granny   33.
Crick, Rev.   17.
Cricket   76, 88, 95-96.

Customs House   22.
Cutler, Mr.   59.

D

D-Day   116.
Damon, Richard   86, 107.
Davis, George   26.
Davis, Harry   26.
Davis, Tommy   52.
Dean Park   76.
Dean, Mr.   44-45.
Denmark Road   9.
Dinevan, Mrs.   46.
Dobell, Mr.   37.
Dorchester Prison   40.
Dorchester Road   115.
Dorey, Arthur   88.
Dorset Farmers   44.
Dorset Mineral Company   34.
Dorset Pottery   11.
Dorset Regiment   76.
Drum Druid   114.
Dunkirk   100, 102.
Durdle Door   90, 100.

E

East Quay Road   79, 88.
Eastlake   65.
Edwards, Syd   86.
Elsdon, Leslie   87.
Emberley, Tinker   26.
Eyers, Jack   88.

F

Fair	60-62.
Fernside Road	44, 65, 77, 92.
Ferry Road	26.
Fire Brigade	33-39, 112.
Fish Street	33, 38.
Fishing	28-30, 91, 114, 124-128.
Fontmell Magna	103.
Football	16, 65, 75-76.
Fossils	127.
French onion men	21, 37, 119.

G

Gallagher, Mr.	60.
General Strike	76-77.
Gilham, Gertie	82-83.
Glassey, Alex	48-49.
Goathorn	22.
Godwin's Slaughterhouse	26-27.
Gondolier Boats	89.
Gough, Trumpy	89.
Greenlands	99-100.
Guest, Freddy	47-48.
, Major	48.-
Guildhall	9, 18, 36, 47-50, 104.
Gymnasium	16, 76.

H

Half Way Diver	55, 57.
Hall Caine	48.
Halley's Comet	11
Hamworthy	16, 18, 24, 28, 69, 88, 95.
Hamworthy Engineering Company	26, 69-70.
Hamworthy Ferry	22, 26-27.
Hamworthy Road	26.
Hannaford, Margaret	16.
Harbour Hill Road	110.
Harman's	38, 40.
Harvell, Bill	60.
Harvey, Charlie	55.
, James	51, 125.
Harvey's	44, 52, 54, 89.
Haven	28-29, 44, 52, 69, 127.
Haven Hotel	51-52, 89.
Hawkes, Dr. Ewart	57.
Hawkes, J.A.	37.
Heckford Park	9, 45.
Henbury	99, 111-114, 116.
Hibbs, Norman	102.
High Street	18, 37, 43-44, 46, 59, 77, 104.
Hight, Pilot	104.
Hill Street	66.
Hockey, Tom	46.
Hodge, Andy	43.
Hodge, Percy	60.
Holder, Margaret	87.
Holes Bay	114.
Holmes, Mr.	45.
Holton Heath cordite factory	17.
Horne, Dr. Maule	97.
Horse troughs	44.
Houseboat	54-57.
Houses	31-32.
Hunger Hill	64.
Hustler, Ernest	86.

I

Itinerant traders	36-37.

J

James Smith Company 70.
James, Jimmy 126.
Jolly Sailor 26.

K

Keene's 34.
Keene, Dennis 65.
Kendall, Ernest 29.
King Edward VII 11.
George V 11.
George VI 85.
King Street 38, 54.
Kingsbury, Tom 76.
Kinson Pottery 24, 105.

L

Ladies' Walking Field 17, 60.
Lagland Street 10, 33-34, 74.
Lake 18.
Legg, Ernest 80.
Level crossing 43, 104.
Library & museum 14-15.
Lifeboat 24.
Lilliput 89.
Llewellin family 17.
Longfleet Church 10.
Longfleet Congregational
    Church 62.
Longfleet Road 24, 47, 71, 114.
Longfleet Rovers 16.
Longfleet St. Mary's 65, 115.
Lovell, Jack 29.

M

Maiden Castle 58, 99.
Marconi, G. 89.
Market Place 104
Market Street 9, 18, 36, 38-40,
    46, 54, 71, 76.
Marston's Brewery 39.
Martin, Mr. 10.
Matthews, Harry 60, 88.
Matthews, Pat 125.
Mayor-making 47.
Maypole Dairy 18.
Meaby, Mr. 51.
Mentone Road 74.
Mockridge, Mr. 16-17.
Morton's Boots 16, 59.
Mount Street 11.

N

New Orchard 46.
New Street 36, 44.
New Zealand 129-131.
Newfoundland 16, 35.
Newtown 105, 107.
Nicholson, Col. 48.
Norrish, Les 16.
North Road 41, 44.
Norton, John J. 14, 22.

O

Oddfellows Hall 76.
Old Harry Rocks 19, 21, 103,
    125, 127.
Orchard Brothers 29.

P

Palmer, Mr.   64.
Panorama Road   52.
Paradise Street   44.
Park Gates East   41, 44, 64-65.
Parkstone Olympic Club   76.
   Operatic Society   74.
Parish, Canon Okes   10.
Parrot's   34.
Pavely, Ruth   86-87.
Paye, Harry   12, 19.
Petty Sessions   49-50.
Phillips' shop   36.
Phillips, Tommy   38.
Photography   93-94, 99, 122-124,
                      126-127, 129.
Pitt, Sergeant Major   12.
Pitwines   27.
Pleasant Sunday Afternoon   66.
Plymouth Brethren   33.
Police Station   9.
Politics   47-48.
Poole Adult School 40, 46-47, 74-75.
   Bridge   21, 24, 55, 104.
   Cycling Club   60.
   Harbour   22, 26, 28-29, 55-57,
                  73, 89, 98, 100, 127.
   Nomads   76.
   Park   11, 16, 27-28, 33, 44,
              47, 59-60, 64-65, 72, 114.
   Pottery   79-88, 98, 102,
                      107, 119-120.
   Rowing Club   59.
   Town Band   25, 34, 47, 60.
   Wheelers   60.
Poole and East Dorset
   Art Society   128.
   Herald   124.

Poulain, Mr.   52.
Pound Lane   44.
Pound Street   44.
Power, Steve   88.
Prankard, Mr.   11-12.
Public Houses   39.
Pulsford, Henry   69.

Q

Quaker Meeting House   77.
Quay   12, 18-19, 21-28,
                  35, 44, 59, 73, 79,
                  102, 124, 128.

R

Railways   22-24, 27, 41-43.
Rationing   18, 114.
Rattray, Miss   10.
Religion   32, 71.
Rice, Mr.   44.
Round House   24, 36, 44.
Royal Blue Coaches   72.
Russian cannon   114.

S

St. James' Church   47.
St. Mary's Road   115.
Salterns Road   62.
Salvation Army   33-34.
Sandbanks 19, 29-30, 38, 44, 51-55,
              57, 89-90, 92, 103, 125.
   Ferry   52-53.
Sandbanks Road   38, 52.
Schofield, Mr.   44.
Schools   9-14, 16, 48, 74, 128.-
Scottie   52.

Sea View 24, 41.
Seldown 60.
Serpentine Road 10.
Shah of Persia 24, 91.
Shell Bay 29, 52, 89, 127.
Sherrin, Tom 90.
Shippick, Captain 102.
Ships 21-22, 24-25.
   'Ballycorus' 69-70.
   'Bournemouth Queen' 70-71, 90.
   'Brodrick Castle' 25.
   'Emperor of India' 25.
   'Empire Sentinel' 100.
   'Empress' 24.
   'Esso Tioga' 126-127.
   'H.M.S. Flinders' 100.
   'Henford' 70.
   'Hinrich Peters' 98-99.
   'Hop', *'Skip'* & *'Jump'* 25
   'Monarch' 90.
   'Pioneer' 55.
   'Pitwines' 102.
   'Pride of the West' 28.
   'Princess Helena' 25.
   'Royal Sovereign' 102.
   'St. Crispin' 54-57.
   'Stirling Castle' 25.
   'Tweedledee' 25.
   'Tweedledum' 25.
   'Victoria' 25.
   , Concrete 18.
Shipwright's Arms 26, 28.
Shops 33-37, 44-46.
Shore Road 52-53.
Short, Edward 33, 72.
Shutler, Dolph 18, 46.
Simpson's Folly 51, 54.
Skinner Street Congregational
   Church 13, 66, 76.

Smith, H.P. 11-12, 73.
Society of Poole Men 73, 122.
Soper, Jimmy 87-88.
South Road 104.
Southall, Len 60.
Southern Roadways 76.
Stabler, Harold 79-80, 120.
   , Phoebe 80, 120.-
Stadium 60.
Steeplechase 128-129.
Sterte 13, 65, 72, 114.
Stevens, Mr. 44-45.
Stokes, Mr. 47.
Stone, George 64.
Stout, Fred 86.
Strand Street 60.
Strickland, E.E. 83.
Studland 89, 99, 103.
Studt, Jacob 60-62.
Sturminster Marshall 111.
Styring's Brewery 39.
Suffragettes 48-49.
Sunday School 71-72.
Sunderland Flying Boats 100,
   103-104, 110.
Sutton Waldren 103.
Swain, Mr. 44.
Swanage 25, 90, 99.
Sweeney, Mr. 119.

T

Tarrant Rushton 116.
Temperance Hall 64, 66.
Thames Street 36.
Theatre Royal 73-74.
Topp's Corner 33, 35, 45-46, 62.
Town Crier 47.
Towngate Street 12, 14, 39, 43.

Trams   41, 73.
Tucker, Tommy   69.
Tydeman, Bill   57.
Typhoid Epidemic   97.

U

Upton House   17.

V

V.E. Day   116-117.
Valentine, Jack   102.
Van Raalte, Charles   47-48.

W

War   12-13, 17-19,
                          57, 100-117.
Way, Mr.   83.
Way, Phyllis   87.
West Bay   90-91, 127.-
West Quay Road   76.
West Shore   14, 24, 55.

West Street   22, 34, 46, 55, 104.
Westover Road   94, 117.
Weymouth   127-128.
Wheatley, Misses   10.
Wheatley, Mervyn   48.
White, Harry   46.
Whitecliff   13, 27, 33, 44, 110.
Whittle, Arthur   65.
Wilson, Sam   86.
Wimborne Minster   99.
Wimborne, Lady Cornelia,   47
  , Lord   47, 51, 57, 73.
Winter, Mr.   39.
Wireless   66-67
Worsam, Rev. Morley   58.
Wright, Frank   86.

Y

Yeatman's   44.

Z

Zeppelin   18.